ESSENTIAL ASL

The Fun, Fast, and Simple Way to Learn American Sign Language

Martin L.A. Sternberg, Ed.D.

ILLUSTRATIONS BY HERBERT ROGOFF AND EDUSELF

Abridged edition of *American Sign Language*

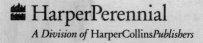

■ HarperPerennial
A Division of HarperCollinsPublishers

To Laura and Bernard Fenster

HarperCollins books may be purchased for educational, business, or sales promotional use. For information, please write to: Special Markets Department, HarperCollins Publishers, Inc., 10 East 53rd Street, New York, NY 10022.

FIRST EDITION

ISBN 0-06-273428-8
96 97 98 99 00 ❖/OPM 10 9 8 7 6 5 4 3 2 1

Contents

Acknowledgments

The original work from which this revised edition is derived, *American Sign Language: A Comprehensive Dictionary,* is the culmination of a period of endeavor that goes back to 1962. Several abridgments and revisions have since appeared. The current work is the latest.

In order to maintain continuity in the evolution of this project, members of the original General Editorial Committee are listed on pages v–vii.

Bringing this project into the Computer Age from its index card and hand-illustrated status has been a major challenge, sometimes a source of trepidation and frustration, but ultimately a unique achievement. This could never have been accomplished without the sustained help and guidance of Kenneth S. Rothschild, my teacher, friend, and major supporter, who not only set up the format for the computer but came to my side countless times to help me out when I was in trouble. Lorri Kirzner gave willingly of her knowledge and expertise to resolve transient difficulties I encountered with the database.

Herbert Rogoff, the talented artist who did the original freehand drawings appearing in editions past—many of which remain among these pages—is thanked yet again.

Robert Wilson, my editor at HarperCollins, is very much the best of a long line of editors under whom I have worked. Thirty-two years is a long time to be affiliated with a single publisher, and Rob's commitment to me and this always-expanding project demonstrates the wisdom of my choice of HarperCollins as my publisher.

Theodora Zavin, literary adviser, has been a reassuring presence throughout the development of the various editions and the production of the CD-ROM versions.

Martin L. A. Sternberg, Ed.D.

General Editorial Committee

(Unabridged Edition)

Editorial Staff

Edna S. Levine, Ph.D., Litt.D., *Project Director.* Late Professor Emeritus, New York University, New York, NY.
Martin L.A. Sternberg, Ed.D., *Principal Research Scientist and Editor-in-Chief.* Adjunct Professor, Adelphi University, Garden City, NY; Adjunct Associate Professor, Hofstra University, Hempstead, NY.
Herbert Rogoff, *Illustrator.* Former Associate Research Scientist, New York University, New York, NY.
William F. Marquardt, Ph.D., *Linguist.* Late Professor of English Education, New York University, New York, NY.
Joseph V. Firsching, *Project Secretary.*

Consulting Committee

Elizabeth E. Benson, Litt.D., *Chief Consultant.* Late Dean of Women and Professor of Speech, Gallaudet University, Washington, DC.
Leon Auerbach, L.H.D., *Senior Consultant.* Late Professor of Mathematics, Gallaudet University, Washington, DC.

Special Consultants

Charles L. Brooks, *Vocational Signs*
Nancy Frishberg, Ph.D., *Editorial*
Emil Ladner, *Catholic Signs*
Max Lubin, *Jewish Signs*
The Rev. Steve L. Mathis III, *Protestant Signs*

Charles Stern, *Foreign Language Consultant*
Mary Ellen Tracy, *Foreign Language Consultant*

Production

Joseph V. Firsching, *Coordinator*
Frank Burkhardt, Ardele Frank, Rosemary Nikolaus,
Bernice Schwartz, Rosalee Truesdale

Editorial Assistants

Jean Calder, *Senior Editorial Assistant*
Lilly Berke, Edna Bock, Nancy Chough, Judith M.
Clifford, Arlene Graham, Pat Rost, Norma Schwartz,
Patrice Smith, Mary Ellen Tracy

Secretarial/Clerical/Typing

Edna Bock, Carole Goldman, Carole Wilkins

Abbreviations

adj.	Adjective
adv.	Adverb, adverbial
adv. phrase	Adverbial phrase
arch.	Archaic
colloq.	Colloquial, colloquialism. Informal or familiar term or expression in sign.
eccles.	Ecclesiastical. Of or pertaining to religious signs. These signs are among the earliest and best developed, inasmuch as the first teachers of deaf people were frequently religious workers, and instruction was often of a religious nature.
e.g.	*Exempli gratia.* L., for example
esp	Especially
i.e.	*Id est.* L., that is
interj.	Interjection
interrog.	Interrogative
L.	Latin
loc.	Localism. A sign peculiar to a local or limited area. This may frequently be the case in a given school for deaf children, a college or postsecondary program catering to their needs, or a geographical area around such school or facility where deaf persons may live or work.
obs.	Obscure, obsolete
pl.	Plural
poss.	Possessive
prep.	Preposition

prep. phrase	Prepositional phrase
pron.	Pronoun
q.v.	*Quod vide.* L., which see
sl.	Slang
v.	Verb
v.i.	Verb intransitive
viz.	*Videlicet.* L., namely
voc.	Vocational. These signs usually pertain to specialized vocabularies used in workshops, trade and vocational classes and schools.
v.t.	Verb transitive
vulg.	Vulgarism. A vulgar term or expression, usually used only in a colloquial sense.

Pronunciation Guide

The primary stress mark (′) is placed after the syllable bearing the heavier stress or accent; the secondary stress mark (′) follows a syllable having a somewhat lighter stress, as in **interrogate** (ĭn tĕr′ ə gāt′).

Symbol	Example	Symbol	Example
ă	add, map	o͝o	took, full
ā	ace, rate	p	pit, stop
â(r)	care, air	r	run, poor
ä	plam, father	s	see, pass
b	bat, rub	sh	sure, rush
ch	check, catch	t	talk, sit
d	dog, rod	th	thin, both
ĕ	end, pet	t͟h	this, bathe
ē	even, tree	ŭ	up, done
f	fit, half	ū	unite, vacuum
g	go, log	û(r)	urn, term
h	hope, hate	yo͞o	use, few
ĭ	it, give	v	vain, eve
ī	ice, write	w	win, away
j	joy, ledge	y	yet, yearn
k	cool, take	z	zest, muse
l	look, rule	zh	vision, pleasure
m	move, seem	ə	the schwa, an un-
n	nice, tin		stressed vowel
ng	ring, song		representing the
ŏ	odd, hot		sound spelled
ō	open, so		*a* in *above*
ô	order, jaw		*e* in *sicken*
oi	oil, boy		*i* in *clarity*
ou	out, now		*o* in *melon*
o͞o	pool, food		*u* in *focus*

Explanatory Notes

Sign Rationale

This term, admittedly imprecise semantically, refers to the explanatory material in parentheses which follows the part of speech. This material is an attempt to offer a mnemonic cue to the sign as described verbally. It is a device to aid the user of the dictionary to remember how a sign is formed.

Verbal Description

The sign and its formation are described verbally. Such terms as "S" hand, "D" position, "both 'B' hands," refer to the positions of the hand or hands as they are depicted in the American Manual Alphabet on page xxiii.

Terms such as "counterclockwise," "clockwise," refer to movement from the signer's orientation. Care should be taken not to become confused by illustrations which appear at first glance to contradict a verbal description. In all cases the verbal description should be the one of choice, with the illustration reinforcing it. The reader should place himself or herself mentally in the position of the signer, *i.e.*, the illustration, in order to assume the correct orientation for signing an English gloss word.

Sign Synonyms

Sign synonyms are other glosses for which the same sign is used. They are found at the end of the verbal description. They are given in SMALL CAPITAL LETTERS.

It is important to remember that the sign synonyms listed do not always carry an equivalent sense in and of themselves. Because meaning for the signer springs from the sign, apparently unrelated glosses can be expressed by similar movements.

Illustrations

A. Illustrations appearing in sequence should not be regarded as separate depictions of parts of a sign. They are fluid and continuous, and should be used in conjunction with the verbal description of a sign, for they illustrate the main features of the sign as one movement flows into the next.

B. Arrows, broken or solid, indicate direction of movement. Again, they are designed to reinforce the verbal description and, where confusion may arise, the reader is cautioned to review the verbal description, always keeping himself or herself mentally in the position of the illustration (the signer).

C. As a general rule, a hand drawn with dotted or broken lines indicates the sign's initial movement or position of the hand. This is especially true if a similar drawing appears next to it using solid lines. This indicates terminal position in the continuum.

D. Groups of illustrations have been arranged as far as possible in visually logical order. They are read from left to right, or from top to bottom. Where confusion is possible, they have been captioned with letters A, B, C, etc.

E. Small lines outlining parts of the hand, especially when they are repeated, indicate small, repeated, or wavy or jerky motions, as described in the verbal section of an entry. .

F. Arrows drawn side by side but pointing in opposite directions indicate repeated movement, as described in the verbal section of an entry.

G. Illustrations giving side or three-quarter views have been so placed to afford maximum visibility and to avoid foreshortening problems. The user of the dictionary should not assume a similar orientation when making the sign. As a general rule, the signer faces the person he or she is signing to.

H. Inclusion of the head in the figures permits proper orientation in the formation of certain signs. The head is omitted where there is no question of ambiguity.

American Manual Alphabet

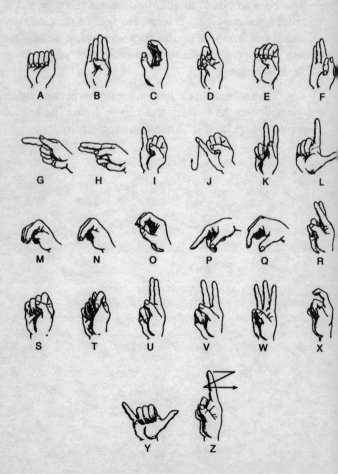

A

ABOUT 1 (ə bout′), *prep*. (Revolving about.) The left hand is held at chest height, all fingers extended and touching the thumb, and all pointing to the right. The right index finger circles about the left fingers several times.

ACCEPT (ăk sĕpt′), *v*., -CEPTED, -CEPTING. (A taking of something unto oneself.) Both open hands, palms down, are held in front of the chest. They move in unison toward the chest, where they come to rest, all fingers closed.

ACROSS (ə krôs′, ə krŏs′), *prep.*, *adv.* (A crossing over.) The left hand is held before the chest, palm down and fingers together. The right hand, fingers together, glides over the left, with the right little finger touching the top of the left hand.

ADD *v.* (Adding on.) The index and middle fingers of the right "H" hand, palm up, are swung up and over until they come to rest on the index and middle fingers of the left "H" hand, held palm down. *Also* RAISE.

ADDRESS (ăd′ rĕs), *n.*, *v*, -DRESSED, -DRESSING. (Same rationale as for LIFE 1, with the initials "L".) The upturned thumbs of the "A" hands move in unison up the chest. *Also* ALIVE, LIFE, LIVE, LIVING.

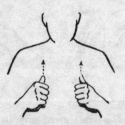

ADVICE (ăd vīs′), *n.* (Take something, *advice*, and disseminate it.) The left hand, held limp in front of the body, has its fingers pointing down. The fingers of the right hand, held all together, are placed on the top of the left hand, and then move forward, off the left hand, assuming a "5" position, palm down.

AFRAID (ə frād′), *adj.* (The heart is suddenly covered with fear.) Both hands, fingers together, are placed side by side, palms facing the chest. They quickly open and come together over the heart, one on top of the other. *Also* FRIGHT.

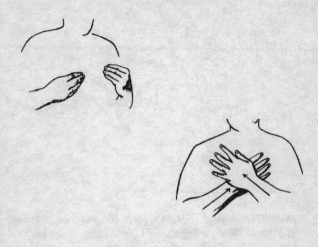

AFTERNOON (ăf′ tər nōōn′, ăf′ -), *n., adj.* (The sun is midway between zenith and sunset.) The right arm, fingers together and pointing forward, rests on the back of the left hand, its fingers also together and pointing somewhat to the right. The right arm remains in a position about 45° from the vertical.

AGAIN (ə gĕn'), *adv*. The left hand, open in the "5" position, palm up, is held before the chest. The right hand, in the right-angle position, fingers pointing up, arches over and into the left palm.

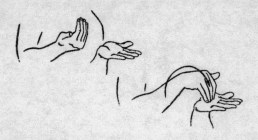

AGAINST (ə gĕnst', -gãnst'), *prep*. (Opposed to; restraint.) The tips of the right fingers, held together, are thrust purposefully into the open left palm, whose fingers are also together and pointing forward. *Also* OPPOSE.

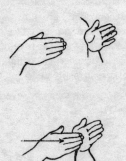

AGREE (ə grē), *v.*, -GREED, -GREEING. (Of the same mind; thinking the same way.) The index finger of the right "D" hand, palm back, touches the forehead (the modified sign for THINK, *q.v.*), and then the two index fingers, both in the "D" position, palms down, are brought together so they are side by side, pointing away from the body (the sign for SAME).

AIRPLANE (âr′ plān′), *n.* (The wings of the airplane.) The "Y" hand, palm down and drawn up near the shoulder, moves forward, up and away from the body several times. Either hand may be used. *Also* FLY.

ALL ALONG (ə lông′, əlŏng′), *adv. phrase*. (From a point up and over.) In the "D" position, palms down, both index fingers touch the right shoulder and then are brought up and over, ending in a palm-up position, pointing straight ahead of the body.

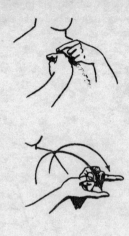

ALLOW (ə lou′), *v.*, -LOWED, -LOWING. (A permissive upswinging of the hands, as if giving in.) Both hands, palms facing and fingers pointing away from the body, are held at chest level, almost a foot apart. With an upward movement, using their wrists as pivots, the hands sweep up until the fingers point almost straight up. *Also* MAY, PERMISSION

ALL RIGHT (rīt), *phrase*. (A straightening out.) The right hand, fingers together and palm facing left, is placed in the upturned left palm, whose fingers point away from the body. The right hand slides straight out along the left palm, over the left fingers, and stops with its heel resting on the left finger-tips. *Also* RIGHT.

ALONE (ə lōn′), *adj*. (One, wandering around in a circle.) The index finger, pointing straight up, palm facing the body (the number *one*), is rotated before the face in a counterclockwise direction.

ALWAYS (ôl′ wăz, -wĭz), *adv*. (Around the clock.) The index finger of the right "D" hand points outward, away from the body, with palm facing left. The arm is rotated clockwise.

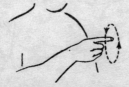

AMERICA (ə mĕr′ ə kə) *n.* (The fences built by the early settlers as protection against the Indians.) The extended fingers of both hands are interlocked, and are swept in an arc from left to right as if encompassing an imaginary house or stockade.

AND (ănd; *unstressed* ənd; ən), *conj.* The right "5" hand, palm facing the body, fingers facing left, moves from left to right, meanwhile closing until all its fingers touch around its thumb.

ANGER (ăn′ gər), *n.* (A violent welling-up of the emotions.) The curved fingers of the right hand are placed in the center of the chest, and fly up suddenly and violently. An expression of anger is worn. *Also* MAD.

ANSWER (ăn′ sər; än´-), *n.*, *v.*, -SWERED, -SWERING.
(Directing a reply from the mouth to someone.) The tip of the
right index finger, held in the "D" position, palm facing the
body, is placed on the lips, while the left "D" hand, palm also
facing the body, is held about a foot in front of the right hand.
The right index finger, swinging around, moves toward and
stops in a pointing position a few inches from the left index
fingertip.

ANY (ĕn′ ĭ), *adj.* The "A" hand, palm down and thumb pointing left, pivots around on the wrist, so the thumb now points
down.

APPLAUD (ə plôd′), *v.*, -PLAUDED, -PLAUDING. (Good words
coming from the mouth; clapping hands.) The fingertips of the
right hand, palm flat and facing the body, are brought up to
the lips, so that they touch (part of the sign for GOOD, *q.v.*).
The hands are then clapped together several times. *Also* CON-
GRATULATE.

APPLE (ăp'əl), *n*. (A chewing of the letter "A" for *apple*.) The right "A" hand is held at the right cheek, with the thumb tip touching the cheek and palm facing out. In this position the hand is swung over and back from the wrist several times, using the thumb as a pivot. The right index knuckle may be substituted for the thumb.

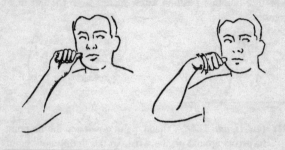

APPOINTMENT (ə point'mənt), *n*. (A binding of the hands together; a commitment.) The right "S" hand, palm down, is positioned above the left "S" hand, also palm down. The right hand circles above the left in a clockwise manner and is brought down on the back of the left hand. At the same instant both hands move down in unison a short distance. *Also* RESERVATION.

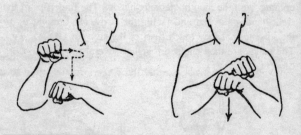

ARRANGE (ə rănj'), *v*., -RANGED, -RANGING. (Placing things in order.) The hands, palms facing, fingers together and pointing away from the body, are positioned at the left side and held about a foot apart. With a slight up-down motion, as if describing waves, the hands travel in unison from left to right. *Also* READY.

ARRIVAL (ə rī′ vəl), *n*. (Arrival at a designated place.) The right hand, palm facing the body and fingers pointing up, is brought forward from a position near the right shoulder and placed in the upturned palm of the left hand (the designated place).

ASHAMED (ə shămd′), *adj*. (The color rises in the cheek; an attempt is made to hide the head.) The backs of the fingers of the right hand, held in the right angle position, are placed against the right cheek. The hand moves up along the cheek, pivoting at the wrist, so that the fingers finally point to the rear.

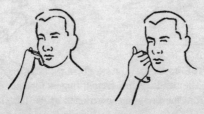

ASK (ăsk, äsk), *v.*, ASKED, ASKING. (Pray tell.) Both hands, held upright about a foot in front of the chest, with palms facing and fingers pointing straight up, are positioned about a foot apart. Moving toward the chest, they come together until they touch, as if in prayer.

ASLEEP (ə slēp′), *adv.* (The eyes are closed.) The fingers of the right open hand, facing the forehead, are placed on the forehead. The hand moves down and away from the head, with the fingers closing so that they all touch. The eyes meanwhile close, and the head bows slightly, as in sleep. *Also* SLEEP.

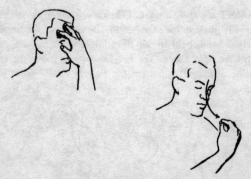

ASSIST (ə sĭst′), *n., v.,* -SISTED, -SISTING. (Helping up; supporting.) The left "S" hand, thumb side up, rests in the open right palm. In this position the left hand is pushed up a short distance by the right.

ATTEMPT (ə tĕmpt′), *n., v.,* -TEMPTED, -TEMPTING. (Trying to push through.) The "A" hands, palms facing before the body, are swung around and a bit down, so that the palms now face out. The movement indicates an attempt to push through a barrier.

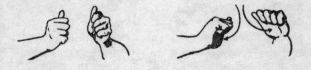

ATTRACT (ə trăkt′), *v.,* -TRACTED, -TRACTING. (Bringing everything together, to one point.) The open "5" hands, palms down and held at chest level, draw together until all the fingertips touch.

AUNT (ănt, änt), *n*. (A female, defined by the letter "A") The "A" hand, thumb near the right jawline (see sign for FEMALE), quivers back and forth several times.

AUTOMOBILE (ô' tə mə bēl´, ô' tə mō' bēl, -mə bēl'), *n*. (The steering wheel.) The hands grasp an imaginary steering wheel and manipulate it.

AUTUMN (ô' təm), *n*. (A chopping down during harvest time.) The right hand, fingers together and palm facing down, makes several chopping motions against the left elbow, to indicate the felling of growing things in autumn.

AWAKE (ə wāk′),*v., adj.*, -WOKE OR -WAKED, -WAKING.
(Opening the eyes.) Both hands are closed, with thumb and
index finger of each hand held together, extended, and placed
at the corners of the closed eyes. Slowly they separate, and the
eyes open.

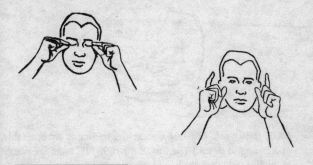

<hr />

AWFUL (ô′ fəl) *adj.* (Throwing out the hands.) Both hands,
their fingertips touching their respective thumbs, are held,
palms facing each other, near the temples. They are thrown out
before the face, assuming "5" positions, palms still facing.

B

BABY (bā′ bĭ), *n.*, *adj.*, *v.*,-BIED, -BYING. (The rocking of the baby.) The arms are held with one resting on the other, as if cradling a baby. They rock from side to side.

BAD (băd), *adj.* (Tasting something, finding it unacceptable, and turning it down.) The tips of the right "B" hand are placed at the lips, and then the hand is thrown down.

BANANA (bə nan′ ə), *n.* (The natural sign.) Go through the motions of peeling a banana, the left index representing the banana and the right fingertips pulling off the skin.

BASEBALL (bās′ bôl′), *n*. (Swinging a bat.) Both "S" hands, the right behind the left, grip an imaginary bat and move back and forth over the right shoulder, as if preparing to hit a baseball. *Also* HIT.

BASKETBALL (băs′ kĭt bôl′), *n*. (Shooting a basket.) Both open hands are held with fingers pointing down and somewhat curved, as if grasping a basketball. From this position the hands move around and upward, as if to shoot a basket.

BATH (băth, bäth), *n*. (The natural sign.) The closed hands move up and down against the chest as if scrubbing it.

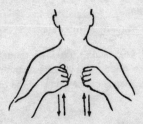

BE (bē; unstressed bǐ), *v.*, BEEN, BEING. (Part of the verb to BE.) The tip of the right index finger, held in the "D" position, palm facing left, is held at the lips, and the hand moves straight out and away from the lips.

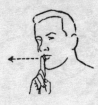

BEAUTIFUL (bū' tə fəl), *adj.* (Literally, a good face.) The right hand, fingers closed over the thumb, is placed at or just below the lips (indicating a tasting of something GOOD, *q.v.*). It then describes a counterclockwise circle around the face, opening into the "5" position, to indicate the whole face. At the completion of the circling movement the hand comes to rest in its initial position, at or just below the lips.

BECAUSE (bǐ kôz', -kŏz'), *conj.* (A thought or knowledge uppermost in the mind.) The fingers of the right hand or the index finger, are placed on the center of the forehead, and then the hand is brought strongly up above the head, assuming the "A" position, with thumb pointing up. *Also* FOR.

BED (bĕd), *n.* (A sleeping place with four legs.) The head is tilted to one side, with the cheek resting in the palm, to represent the head on a pillow. Both index fingers, pointing down, move straight down a short distance, in unison (the two front legs of the bed), and then are brought up slightly, and move down again a bit closer to the body (the rear legs).

BEFORE (bĭ fôr'), *adv.* (One hand precedes the other). The left hand is held before the body, fingers together and pointing to the right. The right hand, fingers also together, and pointing to the left, is placed so that its back rests in the left palm. The right hand moves rather quickly toward the body. The sign is used as an indication of time or of precedence: *He arrived before me.*

BEGIN (bĭ gĭn'), v., -GAN, -GUN, -GINNING. (Turning a key to open up a new venture.) The right index finger, resting between the left index and middle fingers, executes a half turn, once or twice.

BELIEF (bĭ lēf'), n. (A thought clasped onto.) The index finger touches the middle of the forehead (where the thought lies), and then both hands are clasped together.

BELONG (bĭ lông', -lŏng'), v., -LONGED, -LONGING. (Joining together.) Both hands, held in the modified "5" position, palms out, move toward each other. The thumbs and index fingers of both hands then connect. *Also* JOIN.

BE QUIET 1 (kwī´ ət), *v. phrase.* (The natural sign.) The index finger is brought up against the pursed lips.

BETTER (bet´ ər), *adj.* (More good.) The fingertips of one hand are placed at the lips, as if tasting something (*cf.* GOOD). Then the hand is moved up to a position just above the head, where it assumes the "A" position, thumb up. This latter position, less high up than the one indicated in BEST, denotes the comparative degree.

BICYCLE (bī´ sə kəl), *n., v.,* -CLED, -CLING. (The motion of the feet on the pedals.) Both hands, in the "S" position, rotate alternately before the chest.

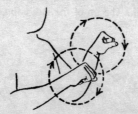

BIRD (bûrd), *n.* (The shape and movement of a beak.) The right thumb and index finger are placed against the mouth, pointing straight out. They open and close.

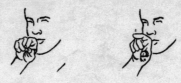

BIRTHDAY (bûrth' dā´), n. The sign for BIRTH is made, followed by the sign for DAY: The left arm, held horizontally, palm down, represents the horizon. The right elbow rests on the back of the left hand, with the right arm in a perpendicular position. The right "D" hand, palm facing left, moves in an arc to the left until it is just above the left elbow.

BLACK (blăk), *adj.* (The darkest part of the face, *i.e.,* the brow, is indicated.) The tip of the index finger moves along the eyebrow.

BLEED (blēd), *v.,* BLED, BLEEDING, *adj.* (Blood trickles down from the hand.) The left "5" hand is held palm facing the body and fingertips pointing right. The right "5" hand touches the back of the left and moves down, with the right fingers wiggling.

BLUE (blōō), *n., adj.* (The letter "B.") The right "B" hand shakes slightly, pivoted at the wrist.

BOAT (bōt), *n.* (The shape; the bobbing on the waves.) Both hands are cupped together to form the hull of a boat. They move forward in a bobbing motion.

BOOK (bŏŏk), *n.* (Opening a book.) The open hands are held together, fingers pointing away from the body. They open with little fingers remaining in contact, as in the opening of a book.

BORING 1 (bôr′ ĭng), *adj.* (The nose is pressed, as if to a grindstone wheel.) The right index finger touches the tip of the nose, as a bored expression is assumed. The right hand is sometimes pivoted back and forth slightly, as the fingertip remains against the nose.

BORN (bôrn), *adj.* (The baby is brought forth from the womb.) Both cupped hands, palms facing the body, are placed at the stomach or lower chest, one on top of the other. Both hands are moved out and away from the body in unison, describing a small arc.

BOTH (bōth), *adj., pron.* (Two fingers are drawn together.) The right "2" hand, palm facing the body, is drawn down through the left "C" hand. As it does, the right index and middle fingers come together.

BOY (boi), *n.* (A modification of the MALE root sign.) The right hand, palm down, is held at the forehead. The fingers open and close once or twice.

BRAVE (brăv), *adj., n., v.,* BRAVED, BRAVING. (Strength emanating from the body.) Both "5" hands are placed palms against the chest. They move out and away, forcefully, closing and assuming the "S" position. *Also* HEALTH.

BREAD (brĕd), *n.* (Act of cutting a loaf of bread.) The left arm is held against the chest, representing a loaf of bread. The little finger edge of the right hand is drawn down over the back of the left hand several times, to indicate the cutting of slices.

BRING (brĭng), *v.*, BROUGHT, BRINGING. (Carrying something over.) Both open hands, palms up, move in an arc from left to right, as if carrying something from one point to another. *Also* CARRY.

BROTHER (brŭth′ ər), *n.* (A male who is the same, *i.e.*, from the same family.) The root sign for MALE is made: The thumb and extended fingers of the right hand are brought up to grasp an imaginary cap brim, representing the tipping of caps by men in olden days. Then the sign for SAME is made: The out-stretched index fingers are brought together, either once or several times.

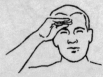

BROWN (broun), *adj.* The "B" hand is placed against the face, with the index finger touching the upper cheek. The hand is then drawn straight down the cheek.

BUT (bŭt; *unstressed* bət), *conj.* (A divergence or a difference; the opposite of SAME, *q.v.*) The index fingers of both "D" hands, palms facing down, are crossed near their tips. The hands are drawn apart.

BUY (bī), *n., v.,* BOUGHT, BUYING. (Giving out money.) The sign for MONEY is made: The upturned right hand, grasping some imaginary bills, is brought down into the upturned left palm, and then the right hand moves forward and up in a small arc, opening up as it does.

C

CAKE (kāk), *n.* (The rising of the cake.) The fingertips of the right "5" hand are placed in the upturned left palm. The right rises slowly an inch or two above the left.

CAN (kăn, kən),*v.* (An affirmative movement of the hands, likened to a nodding of the head, to indicate ability or power to accomplish something.) Both "A" hands, held palms down, move down in unison a short distance before the chest. *Also* MAY.

CARRY (kăr´ ĭ), *v.*, -RIED, -RYING. (Act of conveying an object from one point to another.) The open hands are held palms up before the chest on the right side of the body. Describing an arc, they move up and forward in unison.

CAT (kăt), *n.* (The whiskers.) The thumbs and index fingers of both hands stroke an imaginary pair of whiskers at either side of the face. Also one hand may be used in place of two for the stroking of the whiskers.

CENT (sĕnt), *n.* (The Lincoln head.) The right index finger touches the right temple and moves up and away quickly. This is "one cent." For two cents, the "2" hand is used, etc.

CHANGE (chănj), *n., v.,* CHANGED, CHANGING. (The position of the hands is altered.) Both "A" hands, thumbs up, are held before the chest, several inches apart. The left hand is pivoted over so that its thumb points to the right. Simultaneously, the right hand is moved up and over the left, describing a small arc, with its thumb pointing to the left.

CHASE (chās), *v.*, CHASED, CHASING. (The natural sign.) The "A" hands are held in front of the body, with the thumbs facing forward, the right palm facing left and the left palm facing right. The left hand is held slightly ahead of the right; it then moves forward in a straight line while the right hand follows after, executing a circular motion or swerving back and forth, as if in pursuit.

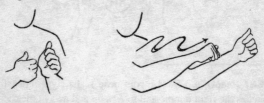

CHEAP (chēp), (*colloq.*), *adj.* (A flip movement indicating of no consequence.) The right fingertips slap the little finger edge of the upturned left hand.

CHEER (chĭr), *n.* (Waving of flags.) Both upright hands, grasping imaginary flags, wave them in small circles.

CHEERFUL (chĭr´ fəl), *adj.* (A crinkling-up of the face.) Both hands, in the "5" position, palms facing back, are placed on either side of the face. The fingers wiggle back and forth, while a pleasant, happy expression is worn. *Also* FRIENDLY.

CHEESE (chēz), *n.* (The pressing of cheese.) The base of the downturned right hand is pressed against the base of the upturned left hand, and the two rotate back and forth against each other.

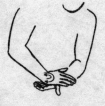

CHEWING GUM (chōō´ ing gum), *n.* (The chewing motion.) The thumb of the right "A" hand, held against the right cheek, swivels forward and back several times. Alternatively, the tips of the right "V" hand are placed at the right cheek and bend in and out. *Also* GUM.

CHILD (chīld), *n.* (The child's height.) The downturned right palm is extended before the body, as if resting on a childs head.

CHILDREN (chǐl´ drən), *n.* (Indicating different heights of children; patting the children on their heads.) The downturned right palm, held before the body, executes a series of movements from left to right, as if patting a number of children on their heads.

CHOCOLATE (chôk´ lit), *n.* (The letter "C"; the icing on the cake.) The right "C" hand makes a counterclockwise circle on the downturned left hand.

CHOOSE (chōōz), *v.*, CHOSE, CHOSEN, CHOOSING. (Taking unto oneself.) The right hand, palm out, is extended before the chest, index finger and thumb in an open position, the other fingers separated and pointing up. The hand is drawn in toward the chest, and the index and thumb close at the same time, indicating something taken to oneself.

CITY (sǐt´ ǐ), *n.* (A collection of rooftops.) The fingertips of both hands are joined, the hands and arms forming a pyramid. The fingertips separate and rejoin a number of times. Both arms may move a bit from left to right each time the fingertips separate and rejoin. *Also* COMMUNITY.

CLASS (klăs, kläs), *n.* (A grouping together.) Both "C" hands, palms facing, are held a few inches apart at chest height. They are swung around in unison, so that the palms now face the body. *Also* ORGANIZATION.

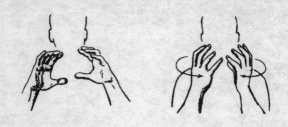

CLEAN (klēn), *adj.* (Everything is wiped off the hand, to emphasize an uncluttered or clean condition.) The right hand slowly wipes the upturned left palm, from wrist to fingertips.

CLOSE 1 (klōs) *v.* (klōs; *v.* klōz), CLOSED, CLOSING. (The act of closing.) Both "B" hands, held palms out before the body, come together with some force.

CLOTHES (klōz, klōᵗȟz), *n. pl.* (Draping the clothes on the body.) With fingertips resting on the chest, both hands move down simultaneously. The action is repeated. *Also* DRESS.

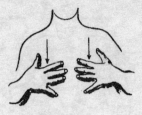

COAT (kōt), *n.* (The lapels are outlined.) The tips of the "A" thumbs outline the lapels of the coat.

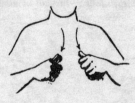

COFFEE (kôf´ ĭ, kŏf´ ĭ), *n.* (Grinding the coffee beans.) The right "S" hand, palm facing left, rotates in a counterclockwise manner, atop the left "S" hand, palm facing right.

COLD (kōld), *adj.* (The trembling from cold.) Both "S" hands, palms facing, are placed at the sides of the body. In this position the arms and hands shiver.

COLLEGE (kŏl´ ĭj), *n.* (Above ordinary school.) The sign for SCHOOL, *q.v.*, is made, but without the clapping of hands. The upper hand swings up in an arc above the lower. The upper hand may form a "C," instead of assuming a clapping position.

COME 1 (kŭm), *v.*, CAME, COME, COMING. (Movement toward the body.) The index fingers, pointing to each other, are rolled in toward the body.

COMPETE (kəm pēt´), *v.*, -PETED, -PETING. (Two opponents come together.) Both hands are closed, with thumbs pointing straight up and palms facing the body. From their initial position about a foot apart, the hands are brought together sharply, so that the knuckles strike. The hands, as they are drawn together, also move down a bit, so that they describe a "V."

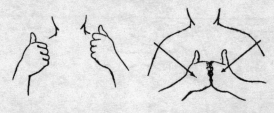

COMPLAIN (kəm plān´), *v.*, -PLAINED, -PLAINING. (The hand is thrust into the chest to force a complaint out.) The curved fingers of the right hand are thrust forcefully into the chest.

COMPLETE (kəm plēt´), *v.*, -PLETED, -PLETING. (Wiping off the top of a container, to indicate its condition of fullness.) The downturned open right hand wipes across the index finger edge of the left "S" hand, whose palm faces right. The movement of the right hand is toward the body.

COMPUTER (kəm pyōō′ tər), *n.* The thumb of the right "C" hand is placed on the back of the left hand and moves up the left arm in an arc.

CONFESS (kən fĕs′), *v.*, -FESSED, -FESSING. (Getting something off the chest.) Both hands are held with fingers touching the chest and pointing down. They are then swung up and out, ending with both palms facing up before the body.

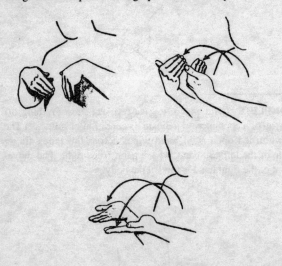

CONGRATULATE *v.* (Shaking the clasped hands in triumph.) The hands are clasped together in front of the face and are shaken vigorously back and forth. The signer smiles.

CONTACT (kŏn´ tăkt), *n., v.,* -TACTED, -TACTING. (The natural movement of touching.) The tip of the middle finger of the downturned right "S" hand touches the back of the left hand a number of times. *Also* FEEL.

CONTINUE (kən tĭn´ ū), *v.,* -TINUED, -TINUING. (Steady, uninterrupted movement.) The "A" hands are held with palms out, thumbs extended and touching, the right behind the left. In this position the hands move forward in a straight, steady line. *Also* LAST, PERMANENT, REMAIN.

CONTRAST (*n.* kŏn´ trăst; *v.* kən trăst´), -TRASTED, -TRAST-ING. (Separateness.) The tips of the extended index fingers touch before the chest, the right finger pointing left and the left finger pointing right. The fingers then draw apart sharply to either side.

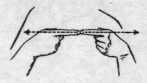

CONVERSATION (kŏn´ vər sā´ shən), *n.* (Movement forward from, and back to, the mouth.) The tips of both index fingers, held pointing up, move alternately forward from, and back to, the lips.

COOK (kŏŏk), *n., v.,* COOKED, COOKING. (Turning over a pancake.) The open right hand rests on the upturned left palm. The right hand flips over and comes to rest with its back on the left palm. This is the action of turning over a pancake. The sign for INDIVIDUAL, for a noun, then follows: Both open hands, palms facing each other, move down the sides of the body, tracing its outline to the hips.

COOKIE (koŏk´ ĭ), *n.* (Act of cutting cookies with a cookie mold.) The right hand, in the "C" position, palm down, is placed into the open left palm. It then rises a bit, swings or twists around a little, and in this new position is placed again in the open left palm.

COOL (koōl), *adj., v.,* COOLED, COOLING. (Fanning the face.) Both open hands are held with palms down and fingers spread and pointing toward the face. The hands move up and down as if fanning the face.

COP (kŏp), *(colloq.), n.* (The letter "C" for "cop"; the shape and position of the badge.) The right "C" hand, palm facing left, is placed against the heart.

CORRECT (kə rĕkt´), *adj.* The right index finger, held above the left index finger, comes down rather forcefully so that the bottom of the right hand comes to rest on top of the left thumb joint. *Also* RIGHT.

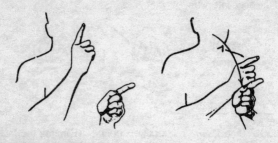

COST (kôst, kŏst), *n.*, *v.*, COST, COSTING. (Nicking into one.) The knuckle of the right "X" finger is nicked against the palm of the left hand, held in the "5" position, palm facing right.

COUNT (kount), *v.*, COUNTED, COUNTING. The thumbtip and index fingertip of the right "F" hand move up along the palm of the open left hand, which is held facing right with fingers pointing up.

COURT (kŏrt), *n.* (The scales move up and down.) The two "F" hands, palms facing each other, move alternately up and down. *Also* JUDGE.

COW (kou), *n.* (The cow's horns.) The "Y" hands, palms facing away from the body, are placed at the temples, with thumbs touching the head. Both hands are brought out and away simultaneously, in a gentle curve.

CRAZY (krā´ zĭ), *adj.* (Turning of wheels in the head.) The open right hand is held palm down before the face, fingers spread, bent, and pointing toward the forehead. The fingers move in circles before the forehead. *Also* INSANE.

CRAZY FOR/ABOUT *phrase*. (Something that makes you dizzy.) The right claw hand, facing the signer, shakes from right to left repeatedly. The mouth is usually held open.

CRY (krī), *v*., CRIED, CRYING. (Tears streaming down the cheeks.) Both index fingers, in the "D" position, move down the cheeks, either once or several times. Sometimes one finger only is used.

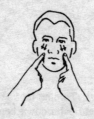

CURIOUS *(colloq.)*, *adj*. (The Adam's apple.) The right thumb and index finger pinch the skin over the Adam's apple, while the hand wiggles up and down.

CUTE (kūt), *adj.* (Titillating to the taste.) The fingertips of the right "U" hand, palm facing the body, brush against the chin a number of times, beginning at the lips. *Also* SUGAR.

D

DAILY (dă′ lǐ), *adj.* (Tomorrow after tomorrow.) The sign for TOMORROW, *q.v.*, is made several times: The right "A" hand moves forward several times from its initial resting place on the right cheek.

DANCE (dăns, däns), *n.*, *v.*, DANCED, DANCING. (The rhythmic swaying of the feet.) The downturned index and middle fingers of the right "V" hand swing rhythmically back and forth over the upturned left palm. *Also* PARTY.

DAUGHTER (dô′ tər), *n.* (Female baby.) The FEMALE prefix sign is made: The thumb of the right "A" hand traces a line on the right jaw from just below the ear to the chin. The sign for BABY is then made: The right arm is folded on the left arm. Both palms face up.

DAY (dā), *n., adj.* (The letter "D"; the course of the sun across the sky.) The left arm, held horizontally, palm down, represents the horizon. The right elbow rests on the back of the left hand, with the right arm in a perpendicular position. The right "D" hand, palm facing left, moves in an arc to the left until it is just above the left elbow.

DEAD (dĕd), *adj.* (Turning over on one's side.) The open hands, fingers pointing ahead, are held side by side, with the right palm down and the left palm up. The two hands reverse their relative positions as they move from the left to the right.

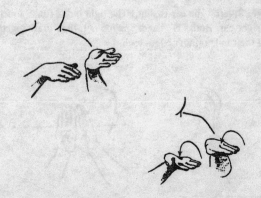

DEAF 1 (dĕf), *adj.* (Deaf and mute.) The tip of the extended right index finger touches first the right ear and then the closed lips.

DEAF 2, *adj.* (The ear is shut.) The right index finger touches the right ear. Both "B" hands, palms out, then draw together until their index finger edges toch.

DECIDE (dǐ sīd′), *v.*, -CIDED, -CIDING. (The mind stops waver-ing, and the pros and cons are resolved.) The right index finger touches the forehead, the sign for THINK, *q.v.* Both "F" hands, palms facing each other and fingers pointing straight out, then drop down simultaneously. The sign for JUDGE, *q.v.*, explains the rationale behind the movement of the two hands here.

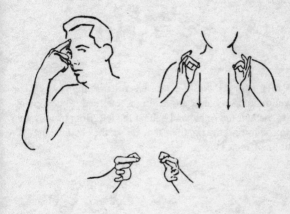

DEFEAT (dǐ fēt′), *v.*, -FEATED, -FEATING. (Forcing the head into a bowed position.) The right "S" hand, placed across the left "S" hand, moves over and down a bit.

DELAY (dĭ lā′), *n.*, *v.*, -LAYED, -LAYING. (Putting off; moving things forward repeatedly.) The "F" hands, palms facing and fingers pointing out from the body, are moved forward simultaneously in a series of short movements.

DEPART (dĭ part′), *v.*, -PARTED, -PARTING. (Pulling away.) The downturned open hands are held in a line, with fingers pointing to the left, the right hand behind the left. Both hands move in unison toward the right. As they do so, they assume the "A" position. *Also* LEAVE.

DESCRIBE (dĭ skrīb′), *v.*, SCRIBED, -SCRIBING. (Unraveling something to get at its parts.) The "F" hands, palms facing and fingers pointing straight out, are held about an inch apart. They move alternately back and forth a few inches.

DESIRE (dĭ zīr'), *n., v.,* -SIRED, -SIRING. (Grasping something and pulling it in.) The upturned "5" hands, held side by side before the chest, close slightly into a grasping position as they move in toward the body. *Also* WANT.

DESTROY (dĭ stroi'), *v.,* -STOYED, -STROYING. (Wiping off.) The left "5" hand, palm up, is held slightly above the right "5" hand, held palm down. The right hand swings up, just brushing over the left palm. Both hands close into the "S" position, and the right is brought back with force to its initial position, striking a glancing blow against the left knuckles as it returns.

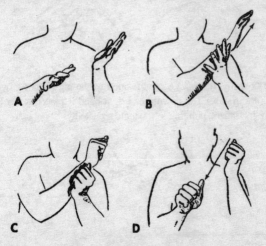

DIFFER (dĭf′ ər), v., -FERED, -FERING. (To think in opposite terms.) The sign for THINK is made: The right index finger touches the forehead. The sign for OPPOSITE is then made: The "D" hands, palms facing the body and index fingers touching, draw apart sharply.

DIFFICULT (dĭf′ ə kŭlt′), adj. (The knuckles are rubbed, to indicate a condition of being worn down.) The knuckles of the curved index and middle fingers of both hands are rubbed up and down against each other. Instead of the up-down rubbing, they may rub against each other in an alternate clockwise-counterclockwise manner. *Also* HARD.

DIRTY (dûr′ tĭ), adj. (A modification of the pig's snout groveling in a trough.) The downturned right hand is placed under the chin. Its fingers, pointing left, wiggle repeatedly.

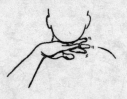

DISAPPEAR (dĭs′ ə pir′), v., -PEARED, -PEARING. (A disappearance.) The right open hand, palm facing the body, is held by the left hand and is drawn down and out, ending in a position with fingers drawn together. The left hand, meanwhile, may close into a position with fingers also drawn together. *Also* GONE.

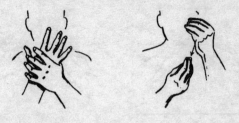

DISAPPOINTED *adj.* (Something sour or bitter.) The right index finger is brought sharply up against the lips, while the mouth is puckered up as if tasting something sour.

DISCO (dis′ kō), *n.* (The natural sign.) The signer mimes dancing to a disco beat.

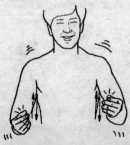

DISCONNECT (dǐs´ kə někt´), *v.*, -NECTED, -NECTING. (An unlocking.) With thumbs and index fingers interlocked initially (the links of a chain), the hands draw apart, showing the break in the chain.

DISCUSS (dǐs kǔs´), *v.*, -CUSSED, -CUSSING. (Expounding one's points.) The right "D" hand is held with the palm facing the body. It moves down repeatedly so that the side of the index finger strikes the upturned left palm.

DISOBEY (dǐs´ ə bā´), *v.*, -BEYED, -BEYING. (Turning the head.) The right "S" hand, held up with its palm facing the body, swings sharply around to the palm-out position. The head meanwhile moves slightly toward the left.

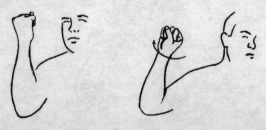

DIVIDE (dĭ vīd'), v., -VIDED, -VIDING. (A splitting apart or dividing.) The two hands are crossed, with the right little finger resting on the left index finger. Both hands are dropped down and separated simultaneously, so that the palms face down.

DIVORCE (dĭ vôrs'), n., v. (The letter "D"; a separating.) The "D" hands, palms facing and fingertips touching, draw apart.

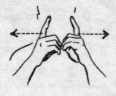

DO (do͞o), v., DOES, DID, DONE, DOING. (An activity.) Both open hands, palms down, are swung right and left before the chest.

DOCTOR (dŏk′ tər), *n.* (The letter "M," from "M.D."; feeling the pulse.) The fingertips of the right "M" hand lightly tap the left pulse a number of times.

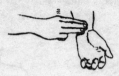

DOG (dôg), *n.* (Patting the knee and snapping the fingers to beckon the dog.) The right hand pats the right knee, and then the fingers are snapped.

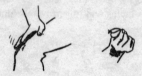

DOLLAR(S) (dŏl′ ər), *n.* (The natural sign; drawing a bill from a billfold.) The right thumb and index finger trace the outlines of a bill on the upturned left palm. Or, the right thumb and fingers may grasp the base of the open left hand, which is held palm facing right and fingers pointing forward; the right hand, in this position, then slides forward along and off the left hand, as if drawing bills from a billfold.

DO NOT *v. phrase.* The thumb of the right "A" hand is placed under the chin. From this position it is flicked outward in an arc. This sign is a variant of DO NOT 1. *Cf.* DON'T 2.

DON'T BELIEVE *v. phrase.* (The nose is wrinkled in disbelief.) The right "V" hand faces the nose. The index and middle fingers bend as a cynical expression is assumed.

DON'T CARE *(colloq.), v. phrase.* (Wiping the nose, *i.e.,* "Keeping the nose clean" or not becoming involved.) The downturned right "D" hand, index finger touching the nose, is suddenly flung down and to the right.

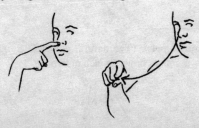

DON'T KNOW *v. phrase.* (Knowledge is lacking.) The sign for KNOW is made: The right fingertips tap the forehead several times. The right hand is then flung over to the right, ending in the "5" position, palm out.

DON'T WANT *v. phrase.* (The hands are shaken, indicating a wish to rid them of something.) The "5" hands, palms facing the body, suddenly swing around to the palms-down position.

DOOR (dôr), *n.* (The opening and closing of the door.) The "B" hands, palms out and edges touching, are drawn apart and then come together again.

DOWN (doun), *prep.* (The natural sign.) The right hand, pointing down, moves down an inch or two.

DREAM (drēm), *n.*, *v.*, DREAMED, DREAMT, DREAMING. (A thought wanders off into space.) The right curved index finger opens and closes quickly as it leaves its initial position on the forehead and moves up into the air.

DRESS (drĕs), *n.*, *v.*, DRESSED, DRESSING. (Draping the clothes on the body.) With fingertips resting on the chest, both hands move down simultaneously. The action is repeated. *Also* CLOTHES.

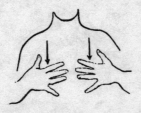

DRINK (drĭngk), *n.*, *v.*, DRANK, DRUNK, DRINKING. (The natural sign.) An imaginary glass is tipped at the open lips.

DRY (drī), *adj.*, *v.*, DRIED, DRYING. (A dryness, indicated by a wiping of the lips.) The "X" finger is drawn across the lips, from left to right, as if wiping them.

DURING (dyŏŏr′ ĭng , dŏŏr′-), *prep.* (Parallel time.) Both "D" hands, palms down, move forward in unison, away from the body. They may move straight forward or may follow a slight upward arc.

E

EACH (ēch), *adj.* (Peeling off, one by one.) The left "A" hand is held palm facing the right. The knuckles of the right "A" hand are drawn repeatedly down the left thumb, from its tip to its base.

EACH OTHER *pron. phrase.* (Mingling with.) Both hands are held in modified "A" positions, thumbs out. The left hand is positioned with its thumb pointing straight up, and the right hand, with its thumb pointing down, revolves above the left thumb in a clockwise direction.

EAR (ĭr), *n.* (The natural sign.) The right index finger touches the right ear.

EARLY (ûr′ lē), *adj.* The middle finger of the downturned right hand rests on the back of the downturned left hand. The top hand moves forward, while the middle finger is drawn back against the palm.

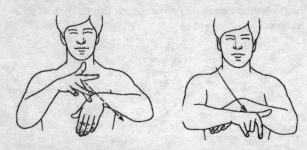

EARTH (ûrth), *n.* (The earth and its axes are indicated.) The downturned left "S" hand indicates the earth. The thumb and index finger of the downturned right "5" hand are placed at each edge of the left. In this position the right hand swings back and forth, while maintaining contact with the left.

EASY (ē′ zĭ), *adj.* (The fingertips are easily moved.) The right fingertips brush repeatedly over their upturned left counterparts, causing them to move.

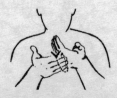

EAT (ēt), *v.*, ATE, EATEN, EATING. (The natural sign.) The closed right hand goes through the natural motion of placing food in the mouth. This movement is repeated.

EDUCATE (ĕj′ ŏŏ kāt′), *v.*, -CATED, -CATING. (Giving forth from the mind.) The fingertips of each hand are placed on the temples. They then swing out and open into the "5" position. *Also* INSTRUCT, TEACH.

EGG (ĕg), *n.* (Act of breaking an egg into a bowl.) The right "H" hand is brought down on the left "H" hand, and then both hands are pivoted down and slightly apart.

ELECT (ĭ lĕkt′), *n.*, *v.*, -LECTED, -LECTING. (Placing a ballot in a box.) The right hand, holding an imaginary ballot between the thumb and index finger, places it into an imaginary box formed by the left "O" hand, palm facing right. *Also* VOTE.

ELECTRIC (ĭ lĕk′ trĭk), *adj.* (The points of the electrodes.) The "X" hands are held palms facing the body, thumb edges up. The knuckles of the index fingers touch each other repeatedly.

ELEVATOR (ĕl′ ə vā′ tər), *n.* (The letter "E"; the rising.) The right "E" hand, palm facing left and thumb edge up, rises straight up.

EMBARRASS (ĕm băr′ əs), *v.*, -RASSED, -RASSING. (The red rises in the cheeks.) The sign for RED is made: The tip of the right index finger of the "D" hand moves down over the lips, which are red. Both hands are then placed palms facing the cheeks, and move up along the face, to indicate the rise of color.

ENCOURAGE (ĕn kûr′ ĭj), v., -AGED, -AGING. (Pushing forward.) Both "5" hands are held, palms out, the right fingers facing right and the left fingers left. The hands move straight forward in a series of short movements.

ENEMY (ĕn′ ə mĭ), n. (At sword's point.) The two index fingers, after pointing to each other, are drawn sharply apart. This is followed by the sign for INDIVIDUAL: Both open hands, palms facing each other, move down the sides of the body, tracing its outline to the hips. *Also* OPPONENT.

ENGAGED (ĕn gājd'), *adj.* (The letter "E"; the ring finger.) The right "E" hand moves in a clockwise circle over the down-turned left hand, and then comes to rest on the left ring finger.

ENJOY (ĕn joi'), *v.*, -JOYED, -JOYING. (A pleasurable feeling on the heart.) The open right hand is circled on the chest, over the heart. *Also* LIKE.

ENOUGH (ĭ nŭf'), *adj.* (A full cup.) The left hand, in the "S" position, is held palm facing right. The right "5" hand, palm down, is brushed outward several times over the top of the left, indicating a wiping off of the top of a cup.

ENTER (ĕn′ tər), *v.*, -TERED, -TERING. (Going in.) The down-turned open right hand sweeps under its downturned left counterpart.

ERROR (ĕr′ ər), *n.* (Rationale obscure; the thumb and little finger are said to represent, respectively, right and wrong, with the head poised between the two.) The right "Y" hand, palm facing the body, is brought up to the chin. *Also* MISTAKE.

ESCAPE (ĕs kāp′), *v.*, -CAPED, -CAPING. (Emerging from a hid-ing place.) The downturned right "D" hand is positioned under the downturned open left hand. The right "D" hand suddenly emerges and moves off quickly to the right.

EXAGGERATE (ĭg zăj′ ə rāt′), (sl.)v., -ATED, -ATING.
(Stretching out one's words.) The left "S" hand, palm facing
right, is held before the mouth. Its right counterpart, palm facing left, is moved forward in a series of short up-and-down
arcs.

EXAMPLE (ĭg zăm′ pəl, -zăm′-), n., v., -PLED, -PLING.
(Directing the attention to something, and bringing it forward.)
The right index finger points into the left palm, held facing out
before the body. The left palm moves straight out.

EXCHANGE (ĭks chānj′), v., -CHANGED, -CHANGING.
(Exchanging places.) The right "A" hand, positioned above the
left "A" hand, swings down and under the left, coming up a bit
in front of it. *Also* REPLACE.

EXCITE (ĭk sīt′), *v.*, CITED, -CITING. (The heart beats violently.) Both middle fingers move up alternately to strike the heart sharply.

EXPECT (ĭk spĕkt′), *v.*, -PECTED, -PECTING. (A thought await- ed.) The tip of the right index finger, held in the "D" position, palm facing the body, is placed on the forehead (modified THINK, *q.v.*). Both hands then assume right angle positions, fingers facing, with the left hand held above left shoulder level and the right before the right breast. Both hands, held thus, wave to each other several times. *Also* HOPE.

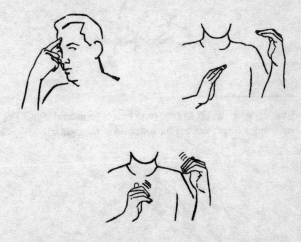

EXPENSIVE (ĭk spěn′ sĭv), *adj.* (Throwing away money.) The right "AND" hand lies in the palm of the upturned, open left hand (as if holding money). The right hand then moves up and away from the left, opening abruptly as it does (as if dropping the money it holds).

EXPLAIN (ĭk splān′), *v.*, -PLAINED, -PLAINING. (Unraveling something to get at its parts.) The "F" hands, palms facing and fingers pointing straight out, are held about an inch apart. They move alternately back and forth a few inches. *Also* DESCRIBE.

EYE (ī) *n.*, *v.*, EYED, EYEING or EYING. (The natural sign.) The right index finger touches the lower lid of the right eye.

EYEGLASSES (ī′ glăs′ əs), *n. pl.* (The shape.) The thumb and index finger of the right hand, placed flat against the right temple, move back toward the right ear, tracing the line formed by the eyeglass frame. *Also* GLASSES.

F

FACE (fās), *v.*, FACED, FACING. (Face to face.) The left hand, fingers together, palm flat and facing the eyes, is held a bit above eye level. The right hand, fingers also together, is held in front of the mouth, with palm facing the left hand. With a sweeping upward movement the right hand moves toward the left, which moves straight up an inch or two at the same time.

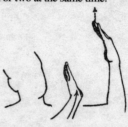

FAIL (fāl), *v.*, FAILED, FAILING. (A sliding.) The right "V" hand, palm up, slides along the upturned left palm, from its base to its fingertips.

FALSE (fôls), *adj.* (Words diverted instead of coming straight, or truthfully, out.) The index finger of the right "D" hand, pointing to the left, moves along the lips from right to left. *Also* LIE.

FAME (fām), *n.* (One's fame radiates far and wide.) The extended index fingers rest on the lips (or on the temples). Moving in small, continuous spirals, they move up and to either side of the head.

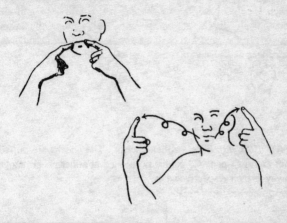

FAMILY (făm′ ə lĭ), *n.* (The letter "F"; a circle or group.) The thumb and index fingers of both "F" hands are in contact, palms facing. The hands swing open and around, coming together again at their little finger edges, palms now facing the body.

FAST (făst), *adj.* (A quick movement.) The thumbtip of the upright right hand is flicked quickly off the tip of the curved right index finger, as if shooting marbles.

FAT (făt), *adj.* (The swollen cheeks.) The cheeks are puffed out and the open "C" hands, positioned at either cheek, move away to their respective sides.

FATHER (fä′ ŧħər), *n.* The thumbtip of the right "5" hand touches the right temple a number of times. The other fingers may also wiggle.

FAX (faks), *n., v.* (The paper coming out.) The downturned left hand undulates a little as it moves under and out of the downturned right hand.

FEEL (fēl), *v.* (The welling up of feelings or emotions in the heart.) The right middle finger, touching the heart, moves up an inch or two a number of times.

FEEL TOUCHED (tǔcht), *v. phrase.* (A piercing of the heart.) The tip of the middle finger of the right "5" hand is thrust against the heart. The head, at the same time, moves abruptly back a very slight distance.

FEMALE (fē′ māl), *n., adj.* (The bonnet string used by women of old.) The right "A" hand's thumb moves down along the line of the right jaw, from ear almost to chin. This outlines the string used to tie ladies' bonnets in olden days. This is a root sign to modify many others. *Viz:* FEMALE plus BABY: DAUGHTER; FEMALE plus SAME: SISTER; etc.

FIGHT 1 (fīt), *n., v.,* FOUGHT, FIGHTING. (The fists in combat.) The "S" hands, palms facing, swing down simultaneously toward each other. They do not touch, however.

FILM (fĭlm), *n.* (The frames of the film speeding through the projector.) The left "5" hand, palm facing right and thumb pointing up, is the projector. The right "5" hand is placed against the left, and moves back and forth quickly. *Also* MOVIES.

FIND (fīnd), *n., v.,* FOUND, FINDING. (The natural motion of selecting something from the hand.) The thumb and index fingers of the outstretched right hand grasp an imaginary object on the upturned left palm. The right hand then moves straight up. *Also* PICK.

FINISH (fĭn' ĭsh), *(colloq.), n., v.,* -ISHED, -ISHING. (Shaking the hands to rid them of something.) The upright "5" hands, palms facing each other, are suddenly and quickly swung around to a palm-out position.

FIRE (fīr), *n., v.,* FIRED, FIRING. (The leaping of flames.) The "5" hands are held with palms facing the body. They move up and down alternately, while the fingers wiggle.

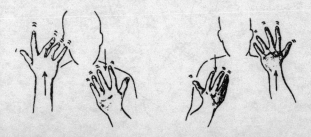

FIRST (fûrst), *adj.* (The first finger is indicated.) The right index finger touches the upturned left thumb.

FLOWER (flou′ ər), *n.* (The natural motion of smelling a flower.) The right hand, grasping an imaginary flower, holds it first against the right nostril and then against the left.

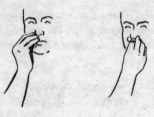

FLUTE (flo͞ot), *n.* (Playing the instrument.) The signer mimes playing a flute.

FLY *v., n.* (The wings are spread.) The downturned hand, thumb, index, and middle fingers extended, moves straight forward.

FOLLOW (fŏl ′ō), *v.,* -LOWED, -LOWING. (One hand follows the other.) The "A" hands are used, thumbs pointing up. The right is positioned a few inches behind the left. The left hand moves straight forward, while the right follows behind in a series of wavy, movements.

FOOLISH (fōō′lĭsh), *adj.* (Thoughts flickering back and forth.) The right "Y" hand, thumb almost touching the forehead, is shaken back and forth across the forehead several times.

FOOTBALL (fŏŏt′ bôl′), *n.* (The teams lock in combat.) The "5" hands, facing each other, are interlocked suddenly. They are drawn apart and the action is repeated.

FOR (fôr), *prep.* (The thoughts are directed outward, toward a specific goal or purpose.) The right index finger, resting on the right temple, leaves its position and moves straight out in front of the face.

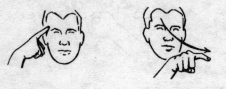

FORBID (fər bĭd′), *v.,* -BADE or -BAD, -BIDDEN or -BID, -BID-DING. The downturned right "D" or "L" hand is thrust forcefully into the left palm.

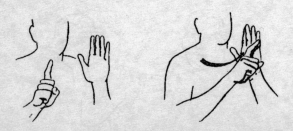

FORGET (fər gĕt′), *v.*, -GOT, -GOTTEN, -GETTING. (Wiping knowledge from the mind.) The right hand, fingers pointing left, rests on the forehead. It moves off to the right, assuming the "A" position, thumb up and palm facing the signer's rear.

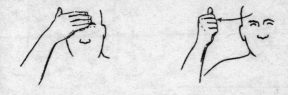

FORGIVE (fər gĭv′), *v.*, -GAVE, -GIVEN, -GIVING. (A wiped-off and cleaned slate.) The right hand wipes off the left palm several times.

FRANKFURTER (The shape in a roll or bun.) The left hand is held with the fingers pointing up. The right index finger is placed between the thumb and the other fingers.

FREE (frē), *adj.*, *v.*, FREED, FREEING. (Breaking the bonds.) The "S" hands, crossed in front of the body, swing apart and face out.

FREQUENT (*adj.* frē′ kwənt; *v.* frĭ kwĕnt ′), -QUENTED, -QUENTING. The left hand, open in the "5" position, palm up, is held before the chest. The right hand, in the right-angle position, fingers pointing up, arches over and into the left palm. This is repeated several times. *Also* OFTEN.

FRIEND (frĕnd), *n.* (Locked together in friendship.) The right and left hands are interlocked at the index fingers. The hands separate, change their relative positions, and come together again as before.

FRIENDLY (frĕnd′ lē), *adj.* (A crinkling-up of the face.) Both hands, in the "5" position, palms facing back, are placed on either side of the face. The fingers wiggle back and forth, while a pleasant, happy expression is worn. *Also* CHEERFUL.

FRIGHT (frīt), *n.* (The heart is suddenly covered with fear.) Both hands, fingers together, are placed side by side, palms facing the chest. They quickly open and come together over the heart, one on top of the other. *Also* AFRAID.

FROM (frŏm), *prep.* (The "away from" action is indicated.) The knuckle of the right "X" finger is placed against the base of the left "D" or "X" finger, and then moved away in a slight curve toward the body.

FUNNY (fŭn' ē), *adj.* (The nose wrinkles in laughter.) The tips of the right index and middle fingers brush repeatedly off the tip of the nose. *Also* HUMOR.

FUTURE (fū′ chər), *n.* (Something ahead or in the future.) The upright, open right hand, palm facing left, moves straight out and slightly up from a position beside the right temple. *Also* LATER.

G

GAME (gām), *n.* (Two individuals pitted against each other.) The hands are held in the "A" position, thumbs pointing straight up, palms facing the body. They come together forcefully, moving down a bit as they do, and the knuckles of one hand strike those of the other.

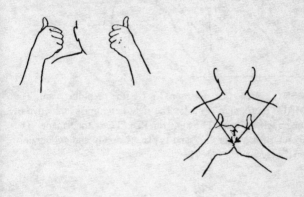

GAS (găs), *n.* (The act of pouring gasoline into an automobile tank.) The thumb of the right "A" hand is placed into the hole formed by the left "O" hand.

GAY (gā), *n., adj.* (Homosexual.) The tips of the "G" fingers are placed on the chin.

GENTLEMAN (jĕn′ təl mən), *n.* (A fine or polite man.) The MALE prefix sign is made: The right hand grasps the edge of an imaginary cap. The sign for POLITE is then made: The thumb of the right "5" hand is placed slowly and deliberately on the right side of the chest.

GET (gĕt), *v.*, GOT, GOTTEN, GETTING. (A grasping and bringing forward to oneself.) Both hands, in the "5" position, fingers curved, are crossed at the wrists, with the left palm facing right and the right palm facing left. They are brought in toward the chest, while closing into a grasping "S" position.

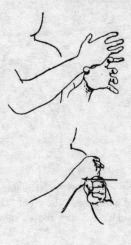

GET UP (ŭp), *v. phrase.* (Getting onto one's feet.) The upturned index and middle fingers of the right hand, representing the legs, are swung up and over in an arc, coming to rest in the upturned left palm. *Also* STAND

GIRL (gûrl), *n.* (A female who is small.) The FEMALE root sign is given: The thumb of the right "A" hand moves down along the line of the right jaw, from ear almost to chin. This outlines the string used to tie ladies' bonnets in olden days. The downturned open right hand is then held at waist level, indicating the short height of the female.

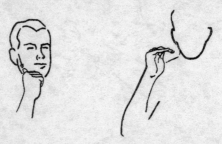

GIVE (gĭv), *v.*, GAVE, GIVEN, GIVING. (Holding something and extending it toward someone.) The right "O" hand is held before the right shoulder and then moved outward in an arc, away from the body.

GIVE ME (mē), *v. phrase.* (Extending the hand toward oneself.) This sign is a reversal of GIVE.

GLAD (glăd), *adj.* (The heart is stirred; the spirits bubble up.) The open right hand, palm facing the body, strikes the heart repeatedly, moving up and off the heart after each strike. *Also* HAPPY, JOY.

GLASSES (glăs′ əs), *n. pl.* (The shape.) The thumb and index finger of the right hand, placed flat against the right temple, move back toward the right ear, tracing the line formed by the eyeglass frame. *Also* EYEGLASSES.

GO *interj., v.* (The natural sign.) The right index finger is flung out, as a command to go. A stern expression is usually assumed.

GOAL (gōl), *n.* (A thought directed upward, toward a goal.) The index finger of the right "D" hand touches the forehead, and then moves up to the index finger of the left "D" hand, which is held above eye level. The two index fingers stop just short of touching.

GONE (gôn, gŏn), *adj.* (A disappearance.) The right open hand, palm facing the body, is held by the left hand and is drawn down and out, ending in a position with fingers drawn together. The left hand, meanwhile, may close into a position with fingers also drawn together. *Also* DISAPPEAR.

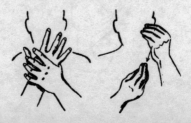

GOOD (good̆), *adj.* (Tasting something, approving it, and offering it forward.) The fingertips of the right "5" hand are placed at the lips. The right hand then moves out and into a palm-up position on the upturned left palm.

GOODBYE (good̆´ bī´), *interj.* (A wave of the hand.) The right open hand waves back and forth several times. *Also* HELLO.

GO TO BED *v. phrase.* (Laying the head on the pillow.) The head is placed on its side, in the open palm, and the eyes are closed.

GOVERNMENT (gŭv′ ərn mənt, -ər-), *n.* (The head indicates the head or seat of government.) The right index finger, pointing toward the right temple, describes a small clockwise circle and comes to rest on the right temple.

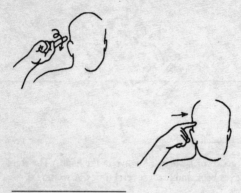

GRANDFATHER *n.* The "A" hands are held with the left in front of the right, and the right thumb positioned against the forehead. Both hands open into the "5" position, so that the right little finger touches or almost touches the left thumb. Both hands may, as they open, move forward an inch or two.

GRANDMOTHER *n.* The "A" hands are positioned as in GRANDFATHER 2 but with the right thumb on the right cheek. They open in the same manner as in GRANDFATHER.

GRAY *adj.* (Intermingling of colors, in this case black and white.) The open "5" hands, fingers pointing to one another and palms facing the body, alternately swing in toward and out from the body. Each time they do so, the fingers of one hand pass through the spaces between the fingers of the other.

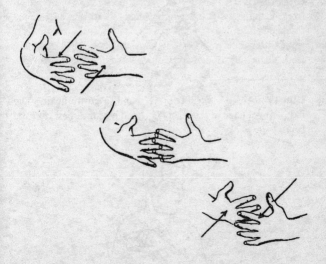

GROW (grō), *v.*, GREW, GROWN, GROWING. (Flowers or plants emerge from the ground.) The right fingers, pointing up, emerge from the closed left hand, and they spread open as they do. *Also* SPRING.

GUIDE (gīd), *n., v.*, GUIDED, GUIDING. (One hand leads the other). The right hand grasps the tips of the left fingers and pulls the left hand forward. *Also* LEAD.

GUILTY (gĭl′ tĭ), *adj.* (The "G" hand; a guilty heart.) The index finger edge of the right "G" hand taps the chest over the heart.

GUM (gum), *n*. (The chewing motion.) The thumb of the right "A" hand, held against the right cheek, swivels forward and back several times. Alternatively, the tips of the right "V" hand are placed at the right cheek and move in and out. *Also* CHEWING GUM.

H

HAIR (hâr), *n.* (The natural sign.) A lock of hair is grasped by the right index finger and thumb.

HAPPY (hăp′ ĭ), *adj.* (The heart is stirred; the spirits bubble up.) The open right hand, palm facing the body, strikes the heart repeatedly, moving up and off the heart after each strike. *Also* GLAD, JOY.

HARD (härd), *adj.* (The knuckles are rubbed, to indicate a condition of being worn down.) The knuckles of the curved index and middle fingers of both hands are rubbed up and down against each other. Instead of the up-down rubbing, they may rub against each other in an alternate clockwise-counterclockwise manner. *Also* DIFFICULT.

HARD OF HEARING *adj. phrase.* (The "H" is indicated twice.) The right "H" hand drops down an inch or so, rises, moves in a short arc to the right, and drops down an inch or so again.

HARM (härm), *n.* (A stabbing pain.) The "D" hands, index fingers pointing to each other, are rotated in elliptical fashion before the chest—simultaneously but in opposite directions. *Also* HURT, INJURE, INJURY, PAIN.

HATE (hāt), *n., v.,* HATED, HATING. (To push away and recoil from; avoid.) The two open hands, palms facing left, are pushed deliberately to the left, as if pushing something away. An expression of disdain or disgust is worn.

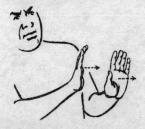

HAVE (hăv), *v.*, HAS, HAD, HAVING. (The act of bringing something over to oneself.) The right-angle hands, palms facing and thumbs pointing up, are swept toward the body until the fingertips come to rest against the middle of the chest.

HAVE TO *v. phrase.* (Being pinned down.) The right hand, in the "X" position, palm down, moves forcefully up and down once or twice. An expression of determination is frequently assumed. *Also* MUST.

HE (hē), *pron.* (Pointing at a male.) The MALE prefix sign is made: The right hand grasps an imaginary cap brim. The right index finger then points at an imaginary male. If in context the gender is clear, the prefix sign is usually omitted. *Also* HIM.

HEADACHE (hĕd′ āk′), *n.* (A stabbing pain in the head.) The index fingers, pointing to each other, move back and forth on the forehead.

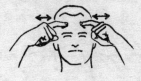

HEALTH (hĕlth), *n.* (Strength emanating from the body.) Both "5" hands are placed palms against the chest. They move out and away, forcefully, closing and assuming the "S" position. *Also* BRAVE.

HEARING (hĭr′ ĭng), *n., adj.* (Words tumbling from the mouth, indicating the old association of being able to hear with being able to speak.) The right index finger, pointing left, describes a continuous small circle in front of the mouth. *Also* SAID, SAY, SPEAK, SPEECH.

HEARING AID *n.* (Behind the ear.) The right curved index finger is hooked onto the right ear, fingertip facing either forward or backward.

HEAVY (hĕv′ ĭ), *adj.* (The hands drop under a weight.) The upturned "5" hands, held before the chest, suddenly drop a short distance.

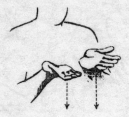

HELLO (hĕ lō′), *interj.* (A wave of the hand.) The right open hand waves back and forth several times. *Also* GOODBYE.

HELP (hĕlp), *n., v.,* HELPED, HELPING. (Helping up; supporting.) The left "S" hand, thumb side up, rests in the open right palm. In this position the left hand is pushed up a short distance by the right. *Also* ASSIST.

HER (hûr), *pron.* (Pointing at a female.) The FEMALE prefix sign is made: The right "A" hand's thumb moves down along the line of the right jaw, from ear almost to chin. The right index finger then points at an imaginary female. If in context the gender is clear, the prefix sign is usually omitted. *Cf.* SHE. For the possessive sense of this pronoun, see HERS.

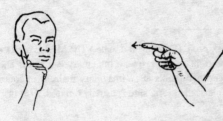

HERE (hǐr), *adv.* The open "5" hands, palms up and fingers slightly curved, move back and forth in front of the body, the right hand to the right and the left hand to the left. *Also* WHERE.

HIDE (hĭd), *v.*, HID, HIDDEN, HIDING. (One hand is hidden under the other.) The thumb of the right "A" hand, whose palm faces left, is placed against the lips. The hand then swings down and under the downturned left hand. The initial contact with the lips is sometimes omitted.

HIM (hĭm), *pron.* (Pointing at a male.) The MALE prefix sign is made: The right hand grasps an imaginary cap brim. The right index finger then points at an imaginary male. If in context the gender is clear, the prefix sign is usually omitted. *Also* HE.

HIPPOPOTAMUS (hip ə pot′ ə məs), *n.* (The large mouth opens.) Both "C" hands are placed on top of each other, fingertips pointing forward. The hands pivot wide open and close again. Another way to make this sign is with the extended index and little fingers of each hand, with the same open-and-close movement as before. The fingers here represent the teeth.

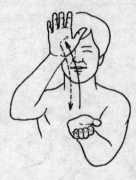

HIT (hĭt), *n., v.,* HIT, HITTING. (The natural sign.) The right "S" hand strikes its knuckles forcefully against the open left palm, which is held facing right.

HOME (hōm), *n.* (A place where one eats and sleeps.) The closed fingers of the right hand are placed against the lips (the sign for EAT), and then, opening into a flat palm, against the right cheek (resting the head on a pillow, as in SLEEP). The head leans slightly to the right, as if going to sleep in the right palm, during this latter movement.

HONEST (ŏn′ ĭst), *adj.* (The letter "H" for HONEST; a straight and true path.) The index and middle fingers of the right "H" hand, whose palm faces left, move straight forward along the upturned left palm.

HONOR (ŏn′ ər), *n., v.,* -ORED, -ORING. (The letter "H"; a gesture of respect.) The right "H" hand, palm facing left, swings down in an arc from its initial position in front of the forehead. The head bows slightly during this movement of the hand.

HOPE (hōp), *n., v.,* HOPED, HOPING. (A thought awaited.) The tip of the right index finger, held in the "D" position, palm facing the body, is placed on the forehead (modified THINK, *q.v.*). Both hands then assume right angle positions, fingers facing, with the left hand held above left shoulder level and the right before the right breast. Both hands, held thus, wave to each other several times. *Also* EXPECT.

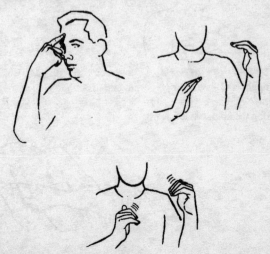

HORSE (hôrs), *n.* (The ears.) The "U" hands are placed palms out at either side of the head. The index and middle fingers move forward and back repeatedly, imitating the movement of a horse's ears. One hand only may be used.

HOSPITAL (hŏs′ pĭ təl), *n.* (The letter "H"; the red cross on the sleeve.) The index and middle fingers of the right "H" hand trace a cross on the upper part of the left arm.

HOUSE (hous), *n*. (The shape of the house.) The open hands are held with fingertips touching, so that they form a pyramid a bit above eye level. From this position, the hands separate and move diagonally downward for a short distance; then they continue straight down a few inches. This movement traces the outline of a roof and walls.

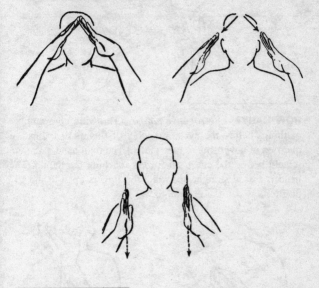

HOW (hou), *adv*. (The hands come into view, to reveal something.) The right-angle hands, palms down and knuckles touching, swing up and open to the palms-up position.

HOW ARE YOU? *phrase.* (What are your feelings?) Both middle fingers quickly sweep up and out from the chest. The eyebrows are raised in inquiry.

HOW MANY? *interrogative phrase.* (Throwing up a number of things before the eyes; a display of fingers to indicate a question of how many or how much.) The right hand, palm up, is held before the chest, all fingers touching the thumb. The hand is tossed straight up, while the fingers open to the "5" position.

HUMOR (hū′ mər, ū´-), *n.* (The nose wrinkles in laughter.) The tips of the right index and middle fingers brush repeatedly off the tip of the nose. *Also* FUNNY.

HURRY (hûr′ ĭ), *v.*, -RIED, -RYING. (Letter "H"; quick movements.) The "H" hands, palms facing each other and held about six inches apart, shake alternately up and down. One hand alone may be used.

HURT (hûrt), *v.*, HURT, HURTING, *n.* (A stabbing pain.) The "D" hands, index fingers pointing to each other, are rotated in elliptical fashion before the chest—simultaneously but in opposite directions. *Also* HARM, INJURE, PAIN.

HUSBAND (hŭz′ bənd), *n.* (A male joined in marriage.) The MALE prefix sign is formed: The right hand grasps the brim of an imaginary cap. The hands are then clasped together.

I *pron.* (The natural sign.) The signer points to himself. *Also* ME.

IGNORANT (ĭg′ nə rənt), *adj.* (The head is struck to emphasize its emptiness or lack of knowledge.) The back of the right "V" hand strikes the forehead once or twice. Two fingers represent prison bars across the mind--the mind is imprisoned.

ILL (ĭl), *adj., n., adv.* (The sick parts of the anatomy are indicated.) The right middle finger rests on the forehead, and its left counterpart is placed against the stomach. The signer assumes an expression of sadness or physical distress. *Also* SICK.

IMAGINATION (ĭ măj′ ə nā′ shən), *n.* (A thought coming forward from the mind, modified by the letter "I" for "idea.") With the "I" position on the right hand, palm facing the body, touch the little finger to the forehead, and then move the hand up and away in a circular, clockwise motion. The hand may also be moved up and away without this circular motion.

IMPORTANT (ĭm pôr′ tənt), *adj.* Both "F" hands, palms facing each other, move apart, up, and together in a smooth elliptical fashion, coming together at the tips of the thumbs and index fingers of both hands.

IMPROVE (ĭm prōōv′), *v.*, -PROVED, -PROVING. (Moving up.) The little finger edge of the right hand rests on the back of the downturned left hand. It moves up the left arm in successive stages, indicating improvement or upward movement.

IN (ĭn), *prep., adv., adj.* (The natural sign.) The fingers of the right hand are thrust into the left. *Also* INSIDE.

IN A FEW DAYS *adv. phrase.* (Several TOMORROWS ahead.) The thumb of the right "A" hand is positioned on the right cheek. One by one, the remaining fingers appear, starting with the index finger. Usually, when all five fingers have been presented, the hand moves forward a few inches, to signify the concept of the future.

INCLUDE (ĭn klōōd'), *v.,* -CLUDED, -CLUDING. (All; the whole.) The left hand is held in the "C" position, fingers pointing right. The right hand, in the "5" position, fingers facing out from the body, palm down, is held above the left. With a horizontal swing to the right, the right hand describes an arc, as the fingers close and are thrust into the left "C" hand, which closes over it.

INDIVIDUAL 1 (ĭn´ də vĭj ´ o͞o əl), *n.* (The shape of an individual.) Both open hands, palms facing each other, move down the sides of the body, tracing its outline to the hips. This is an important suffix sign, that changes a verb to a noun. *E.g.,* TEACH, *v.,* becomes TEACHER, *n.,* by the addition of this sign.

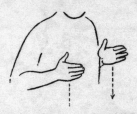

INFORM (ĭn fôrm´), *v.,* -FORMED, -FORMING. (Taking knowledge from the mind and giving it out to all.) The fingertips are positioned on either side of the forehead. Both hands then swing down and out, opening into the upturned "5" position.

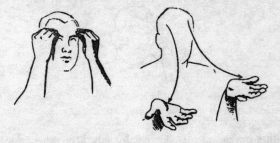

INJURE (ĭn´ jər), *v.,* -JURED, -JURING. (A stabbing pain.) The "D" hands, index fingers pointing to each other, are rotated in elliptical fashion before the chest—simultaneously but in opposite directions. *Also* HARM, HURT, PAIN.

INSANE (ĭn sān'), *adj.* (Turning of wheels in the head.) The open right hand is held palm down before the face, fingers spread, bent, and pointing toward the forehead. The fingers move in circles before the forehead. *Also* CRAZY.

INSECT (ĭn' sĕkt), *(sl.), n.* (The quivering antennae.) The thumb of the "3" hand rests against the nose, and the index and middle fingers bend slightly and straighten again a number of times.

INSIDE (*prep., adv.* ĭn´ sīd'; *adj.* ĭn´ sīd'). (The natural sign.) The fingers of the right hand are thrust into the left. *Also* IN.

INSPIRE (in spīr′), *v.* (The feelings well up.) Both hands, fingers touching thumbs, are placed against the chest, with palms facing the body. They slide up the chest, opening into the "5" position.

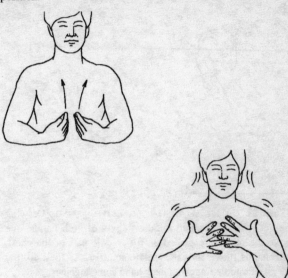

INSTRUCT (ĭn strŭkt′), *v.*, -STRUCTED, -STRUCTING. (Giving forth from the mind.) The fingertips of each hand are placed on the temples. They then swing out and open into the "5" position. *Also* EDUCATE, TEACH.

INTELLIGENT (in tĕl′ ə jənt), *adj.* (The mind is bright.) The middle finger is placed at the forehead, and then the hand, with an outward flick, turns around so that the palm faces outward. This indicates a brightness flowing from the mind. *Also* SMART.

INTEREST (ĭn′ tər ĭst, -trĭst), *n., v.,* -ESTED, -ESTING. (Drawing one out.) The index and middle fingers of both hands, one above the other, are placed on the middle part of the chest. Both hands move forward simultaneously. As they do, the index and middle fingers of each hand come together.

INTERFERE (ĭn′ tər fĭr′), *v.,* -FERED, -FERING. (Obstruct, block.) The left hand, fingers together and palm flat, is held before the body, facing somewhat down. The little finger side of the right hand, held with palm flat, makes one or several up-down chopping motions against the left hand, between its thumb and index finger.

INTERPRET (ĭn tûr′ prĭt), *v.*, -PRETED, -PRETING. (Changing one language to another.) The "F" hands are held palms facing and thumbs and index fingers in contact with each other. The hands swing around each other, reversing their relative positions.

INVITE (ĭn vīt′), *v.*, -VITED, -VITING. (Opening or leading the way toward something.) The open right hand, held up before the body, sweeps down in an arc and over toward the left side of the chest, ending in the palm-up position. Reversing the movement gives the passive form of the verb, except that the hand does not arc upward but rather simply moves outward in a small arc from the body.

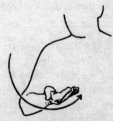

J

JEALOUS (jĕl′ əs), *adj.* (Biting the finger to suppress the feelings.) The tip of the index finger is bitten. The tip of the finger is sometimes used.

JOB (jŏb), *n.* (Striking an anvil.) Both "S" hands are held palms down. The right hand strikes against the back of the left a number of times. *Also* WORK.

JOIN (join), *v.*, JOINED, JOINING. (Joining together.) Both hands, held in the modified "5" position, palms out, move toward each other. The thumbs and index fingers of both hands then connect. *Also* BELONG.

118

JOY (joi), *n.* (The heart is stirred; the spirits bubble up.) The open right hand, palm facing the body, strikes the heart repeatedly, moving up and off the heart after each strike. *Also* GLAD, HAPPY.

JUDGE (jŭj), *n., v.,* JUDGED, JUDGING. (The scales move up and down.) The two "F" hands, palms facing each other, move alternately up and down. *Also* COURT.

K

KARATE (kä rä′ tä), *n.* (The chopping motions.) Using both hands and arms, the signer mimes the chopping motions of karate.

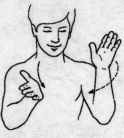

KEEP (kēp), *v.,* KEPT, KEEPING. (Slow, careful movement.) The "K" hands are crossed, the right above the left, little finger edges down. In this position the hands are moved up and down a short distance.

KEY (kē), *n.* (The turning of the key.) The right hand, holding an imaginary key, twists it in the open left palm, which is facing right. *Also* LOCK.

KID (kĭd), *(colloq.), n.* (The running nose.) The index and little fingers of the right hand, held palm down, are extended, pointing to the left. The index finger is placed under the nose and the hand trembles somewhat.

KILL (kĭl), *v.,* KILLED, KILLING. (Thrusting a dagger and twisting it.) The outstretched right index finger is passed under the downturned left hand. As it moves under the left hand, the right wrist twists in a clockwise direction. *Also* MURDER.

KISS (kĭs), *n., v.,* KISSED, KISSING. (Lips touch lips.) With fingers touching their thumbs, both hands are brought together. They tremble slightly, indicating the degree of intensity of the kiss.

KNOW (nō), *v.*, KNEW, KNOWN, KNOWING. (Patting the head to indicate something of value inside.) The right fingers pat the forehead several times.

L

LADY (lā′ dĭ), *n*. (A female with a ruffled bodice; *i.e.*, an elegantly dressed woman, a lady.) The FEMALE root sign is made: The thumb of the right "A" hand moves down along the right jaw, from ear almost to chin. The thumbtip of the right "5" hand, palm facing left, is then placed on the chest, with the other fingers pointing up. Pivoted at the thumb, the hand swings down a bit, so that the other fingers are now pointing out somewhat.

LANGUAGE (lăng′ gwĭj), *n*. The "L" hands, palms facing out, move apart in a wriggling motion, as if spreading out a sentence.

LAST (lăst), *adj.* (The little, *i.e.*, LAST, fingers are indicated.) With the hands in the "I" position, the tip of the right little finger strikes the tip of its left counterpart. The right index finger may be used instead of the right little finger.

LATE (lāt), *adj.* (Hanging back.) The "5" hand and forearm, hanging loosely and straight down from the elbow, move back and forth under the armpit. *Also* NOT YET.

LATER *adj.* (A moving on of the minute hand of the clock.) The right "L" hand, its thumb thrust into the palm of the left and acting as a pivot, moves forward a short distance.

LAUGH (lăf), *n.*, *v.*, LAUGHED, LAUGHING. (The natural sign.) The fingers of both "D" hands move repeatedly up along the jawline, or up from the corners of the mouth. The signer meanwhile laughs.

LAZY (lā' zǐ), *n.* (The initial "L" rests against the body; the concept of inactivity.) The right "L" hand is placed against the left shoulder once or a number of times. The palm faces the body.

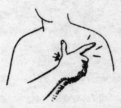

LEAD (lēd), *v.*, LED, LEADING, *n.* (One hand leads the other.) The right hand grasps the tips of the left fingers and pulls the left hand forward. *Also* GUIDE.

LEARN (lûrn), *v.*, LEARNED, LEARNING. (Taking knowledge from a book and placing it in the head.) The downturned fingers of the right hand are placed on the upturned left palm. They close, and then the hand rises and the right fingertips are placed on the forehead.

LEAVE (lēv), *v.*, LEFT, LEAVING. (Pulling away.) The downturned open hands are held in a line, with fingers pointing to the left, the right hand behind the left. Both hands move in unison toward the right. As they do so, they assume the "A" position. *Also* DEPART.

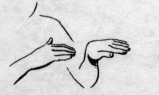

LESBIAN (lez′ bē ən), *n., adj.* (The letter "L.") The right "L" hand is held palm facing the body, index finger pointing left. In this position the hand is placed against the chin.

LESSON (lĕs′ ən), *n.* (A section of a page.) The upturned open left hand represents the page. The little finger edge of the right-angle hand is placed on the left palm near the fingertips. It moves up and over, in an arc, to the base of the left palm.

LETTER (lĕt′ ər), *n.* (The stamp is affixed.) The right thumb is placed on the tongue, and is then pressed into the open left palm.

LIE *n., v.* (Shunting the truth aside.) The index finger edge of the downturned "B" hand moves along the lips (or under the chin) from right to left.

LIFE (līf), *n.* (The fountain [of LIFE, *q.v.*] wells up from within the body.) The upturned thumbs of the "A" hands move in unison up the chest. *Also* ADDRESS.

LIKE (līk), *v.*, LIKED, LIKING. (Drawing out the feelings.) The thumb and index finger of the right open hand, held an inch or two apart, are placed at mid-chest. As the hand moves straight out from the chest the two fingers come together.

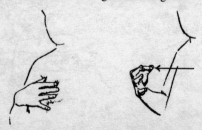

LOCK *(loc.)*, *v.* (Bind down.) The right "S" hand, palm down, makes a clockwise circle and comes down on the back of the left "S" hand, also held palm down.

LONELY (lōn' lĭ), *adj.* ("Oneness"; quietness.) The index finger of the right "1" hand moves straight down across the lips once or twice.

LONG (lông, lŏng), *adj. n., adv.* (The distance is traced.) The right index finger traces a long line along the left arm from wrist almost to shoulder.

LOOK (l͝ook), *v.*, LOOKED, LOOKING. (The eyesight is directed forward.) The right "V" hand, palm facing the body, is placed so that the fingertips are just under the eyes. The hand swings around and out, so that the fingertips are now pointing forward.

LOOK FOR *v. phrase.* (Directing the vision from place to place; the French *chercher.*) The right "C" hand, palm facing left, moves from right to left across the line of vision, in a series of counterclockwise circles. The signer's gaze remains concentrated and his head turns slowly from right to left.

LOSE (l͞ooz), *v.*, LOST, LOSING. (Dropping something.) Both hands, with fingers touching their respective thumbs, are held palms up and with the backs of the fingers almost touching or in contact with one another. The hands drop into an open position, with fingers pointing down.

LOVE (lŭv), *n., v.,* LOVED, LOVING. (Clasping the heart.) The "5" hands are held one atop the other over the heart. Sometimes the "S" hands are used, in which case they are crossed at the wrists.

LOVER (lŭv′ ər), *(colloq.), n.* (Heads nodding toward each other.) The "A" hands are placed together before the body with thumbs up. The thumbs wiggle up and down. *Also* SWEET-HEART.

M

MACHINE (mə shĕn'), *n.* (The meshing gears.) With the knuckles of both hands interlocked, the hands pivot up and down, imitating the meshing of gear teeth.

MAD (măd), *adj.* (A violent welling-up of the emotions.) The curved fingers of the right hand are placed in the center of the chest, and fly up suddenly and violently. An expression of anger is worn. *Also* ANGER.

MAKE (māk), *v.*, MADE, MAKING. *n.* (Fashioning something with the hands.) The right "S" hand, palm facing left, is placed on top of its left counterpart, whose palm faces right. The hands are twisted back and forth, striking each other slightly after each twist.

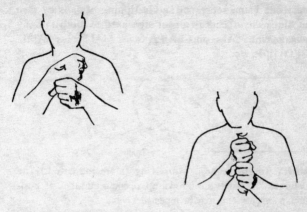

MAKE LOVE *(sl.), v. phrase.* (Necks interlocked.) The "S" hands, palms facing, are crossed at the wrists. They swing up and down while the wrists remain in contact.

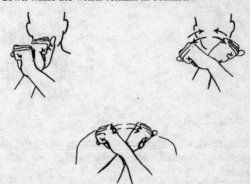

MALE (māl), *n., adj.* (The man's cap.) The thumb and extended fingers of the right hand are brought up to grasp an imaginary cap brim, representing the tipping of caps by men in olden days. This is a root sign used to modify many others. *Viz.:* MALE plus BABY: SON; MALE plus SAME: BROTHER; etc.

MANY (mĕn′ ĭ), *adj.* (*Many* fingers are indicated.) The upturned "S" hands are thrown up, opening into the "5" position, palms up. This may be repeated.

MARRY (măr′ ĭ), *v.* (A clasping of hands, as during the wedding ceremony.) The hands are clasped together, the right on top of the left.

MAY (mā), *v.* (Weighing one thing against another.) The upturned open hands move alternately up and down.

MCDONALD'S (mək don′ ədz), *n.* (The letter "M"; the arches of the well-known hamburger place.) The right "M" hand describes one or two arches along the back of the downturned left hand.

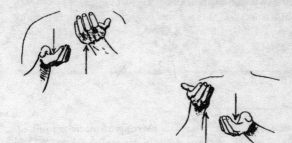

ME (mē; *unstressed* mĭ), *pron.* (The natural sign.) The signer points to himself. *Also* I.

MEAT (mēt), *n.* (The fleshy part of the hand.) The right index finger and thumb squeeze the fleshy part of the open left hand, between thumb and index finger.

MEDICINE (mĕd′ ə sən), *n.* (Mixing of medicine; rolling a pill.) The ball of the middle fingertip of the right "5" hand describes a small counterclockwise circle in the upturned left palm.

MEET (mēt), *v.,* MET, MEETING. (A coming together of two persons.) Both "D" hands, palms facing each other, are brought together.

MEETING (mē′ tǐng), *n.* (Assemble all together.) Both "5" hands, palms facing, are held with fingers pointing out from

the body. With a sweeping motion they are brought in toward
the chest, and all fingertips come together. This is repeated.

MEMORIZE (mĕm′ ə rīz′), *v.,* -RIZED, -RIZING. (Holding on to
knowledge.) The open right hand is placed on the forehead.
Then as it is removed straight forward, it is clenched into a
fist.

MERCY (mûr′ sĭ), *n.* (Feelings from the heart, conferred on
others.) The middle fingertip of the open right hand touches
the chest over the heart. The same open hand then moves in a
small, clockwise circle before the right shoulder, with palm
facing forward and fingers pointing up. *Also* SYMPATHY.

MIGHT (mīt), *n.* (Flexing the muscles.) With fists clenched, palms facing back, the signer raises both arms and shakes them once, with force. *Also* POWER.

MILK (mĭlk), *n., v.,* MILKED, MILKING. (The act of milking a cow.) Both hands, alternately grasping and releasing imaginary teats, move alternately up and down before the body.

MILLION (mĭl′ yən), *n., adj.* (A thousand thousands.) The fingertips of the right "M" hand, palm down, are thrust twice into the upturned left palm, first at the base of the palm and then near the base of the left fingers. (The "M" stands for *mille,* the Latin word for *thousand.*)

MINE (mīn), *pron.* (Pressing something to one's bosom.) The "5" hand is brought up against the chest.

MINUTE (mĭn′ ĭt), *n.* (The minute hand of a clock.) The right "D" hand is held with its index finger edge against the palm of the left "5" hand, which faces right. The right index finger moves forward in a short arc.

MISTAKE (mĭs tāk′), *n.* (Rationale obscure; the thumb and little finger are said to represent, respectively, right and wrong, with the head poised between the two.) The right "Y" hand, palm facing the body, is brought up to the chin. *Also* ERROR.

MISUNDERSTAND (mĭs´ ŭn dər stănd´), *v.*, -STOOD, -STAND-ING. (The thought is twisted around.) The right "V" hand is positioned with index and middle fingers touching the right side of the forehead. The hand swings around so that the palm now faces out, with the two fingers still on the forehead.

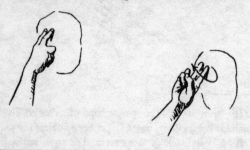

MIX (mĭks), *n.*, *v.*, MIXED, MIXING. (Scrambling or mixing up.) The downturned right hand is positioned above the upturned left. The fingers of both are curved. Both hands move in opposite horizontal circles.

MONEY 1 (mŭn´ ĭ), *n.* (Slapping of paper money in the palm.) The upturned right hand, grasping some imaginary bills, is brought down into the upturned left palm a number of times.

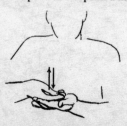

MONTH (mŭnth), *n.* (The tip and three joints represent the four weeks of a month.) The extended right index finger moves down along the upturned, extended left index finger.

MOON (mōōn), *n.* (The face only.) The right "C" hand indicates the face of the moon.

MORE (mōr), *adj., n., adv.* (One hand is added to the other; an addition.) Both hands, palms facing, are held fingers together, the left a bit above the right. The right hand is brought up to the left until their fingertips touch.

MORNING (môr′ nĭng), *n.* (The sun comes over the horizon.)
The little finger edge of the left hand rests in the crook of the
right elbow. The left arm, held horizontally, represents the horizon. The open right hand, fingers together and pointing up, with
palm facing the body, rises slowly to an almost upright angle.

MOTHER (mŭŧh′ ər) (*colloq.*), *n.* (Derived from the FEMALE
root sign.) The thumb of the right "5" hand rests on the right
cheek or on the right chin bone. The other fingers wiggle slightly.
Or the thumb is thrust repeatedly into the right side of the face,
and the rest of the hand remains open and in the "5" position,
palm facing out. This latter modification is used for MAMA.

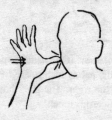

MOVE (mōōv), *n., v.,* MOVED, MOVING. (Moving from one
place to another.) The downturned hands, fingers touching their
respective thumbs, move in unison from left to right. *Also* PUT.

MOVIES (m$\overline{oo}$′ vĭ), *n.* (The frames of the film speeding through the projector.) The left "5" hand, palm facing right and thumb pointing up, is the projector. The right "5" hand is placed against the left, and moves back and forth quickly. *Also* FILM.

MUCH (mŭch), *adj., adv.* (A large amount.) The "5" hands face each other, fingers curved and touching. They move apart rather quickly.

MULTIPLY (mŭl′ tə plī′), *v.,* -PLIED, -PLYING. (A multiplying.) The "V" hands, palms facing the body, alternately cross and separate, several times.

MURDER (mûr′ dər), *n*. (Thrusting a dagger and twisting it.) The outstretched right index finger is passed under the down-turned left hand. As it moves under the left hand, the right wrist twists in a clockwise direction. *Also* KILL.

MUSEUM (myoō zē′ əm), *n*. (The letter "M"; a house or building.) With both hands forming the letter "M," the signer traces the outline of the roof and walls.

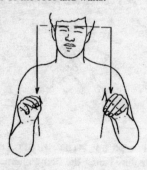

MUSIC (mū′ zĭk), *n*. (A rhythmic, wavy movement of the hand, to indicate a melody; the movement of a conductor's hand in directing a musical performance.) The right "5" hand, palm facing left, is waved back and forth next to the left hand, in a series of elongated figure-eights.

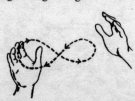

MUST (mŭst), *aux. v.* (Being pinned down.) The right hand, in the "X" position, palm down, moves forcefully up and down once or twice. An expression of determination is frequently assumed. *Also* HAVE TO.

MYSELF (mī sĕlf'), *pron.* (The thumb represents the self.) The upturned thumb of the right "A" hand is brought up against the chest.

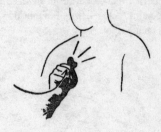

N

NAKED (nā′ kĭd), *adj.* (Devoid of everything on the surface.) The middle finger of the downturned right "5" hand sweeps over the back of the downturned left "A" or "S" hand, from wrist to knuckles, and continues beyond a bit.

NAME (nām), *n., v.,* NAMED, NAMING. (The "X" used by illiterates in writing their names. This sign is indicative of widespread illiteracy when the language of signs first began to evolve as an instructional medium in deaf education.) The right "H" hand, palm facing left, is brought down on the left "H" hand, palm facing right.

NATION (nā′ shən), *n.* (An established area.) The right "N" hand, palm down, executes a clockwise circle above the downturned prone left hand. The tips of the "N" fingers then move straight down and come to rest on the back of the left hand.

NEAR (nĭr), *adv., prep.* (One hand is near the other.) The left hand, cupped, fingers together, is held before the chest, palm facing the body. The right hand, also cupped, fingers together, moves a very short distance back and forth, as it is held in front of the left.

NEPHEW (nĕf' ū), *n.* (The initial "N"; the upper or masculine portion of the head.) The right "N" hand, held near the right temple, shakes slightly or pivots at the wrist.

NERVOUS (nûr' vəs), *adj.* (The trembling fingers.) Both "5" hands, held palm down, tremble noticeably.

NEVER (nĕv′ ər), *adv.* The open right hand, fingers together and palm facing out, moves in a short arc from left to right, and then straight down. The movement is likened to forming a question mark or an "S" in the air.

NEVERTHELESS (nĕv′ ər ŧħə lĕs′), *adv.* Both hands, in the "5" position, are held before the chest, fingertips facing each other. With an alternate back-forth movement, the fingertips are made to strike each other.

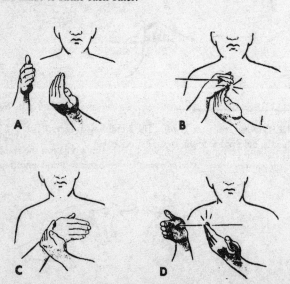

NEW (nū, nōō), *adj.* (Turning over a new leaf.) With both hands held palm up before the body, the right hand sweeps in an arc into the left, and continues up a bit.

NEXT WEEK *adv. phrase.* The upright, right "D" hand is placed palm-to-palm against the left "5" hand, whose palm faces right. The right "D" hand moves along the left palm from base to fingertips and then beyond in an arc.

NEXT YEAR *adv. phrase.* (A year in the future.) The right "S" hand, palm facing left, is brought forcefully down to rest on the upturned thumb edge of the left "S" hand, which is held with palm facing right. (*Cf.* YEAR.) From this position the right hand moves forward with index finger extended and pointing ahead.

NIECE (nĕs), *n.* (The initial "N"; the lower or feminine portion of the head.) The right "N" hand, held near the right side of the jaw, shakes slightly, or pivots at the wrist.

NIGHT (nīt), *n.* (The sun drops beneath the horizon.) The left hand, palm down, is positioned at chest height. The downturned right hand, held an inch or so above the left, moves over the left hand in an arc, as the sun setting beneath the horizon.

NO (nō), *interj.* (The letters "N" and "O".) The index and middle fingers of the right "N" hand are held raised, and are then lowered against the extended right thumb, in a modified "O" position.

NOISE (noiz), *n.* (A shaking which disturbs the ear.) After placing the index finger on the ear, both hands assume the "S"

position, palms down. They move alternately back and forth, forcefully.

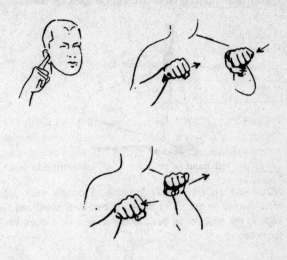

NONE 2, *adj.* (The "O" hands.) Both "O" hands are crossed at the wrists before the chest, thumb edges toward the body. From this position the hands draw apart, the right hand moving to the right and the left hand to the left.

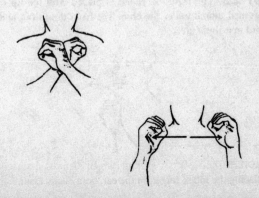

NOON (noon), *n.* (The sun is directly overhead.) The right "B" hand, palm facing left, is held upright in a vertical position, its elbow resting on the back of the open left hand.

NOSY (nō′ zĭ), *(sl.), adj.* (A big nose.) The right index finger, after resting on the tip of the nose, moves forward and then back to the nose, in an oval, as if tracing a long extension of the nose.

NOT *adv.* The right "A" hand is placed with the tip of the upturned thumb under the chin. The hand draws out and forward in a slight arc.

NOTHING (nŭth′ ĭng), *n*. (The zeros.) Both "O" hands, palms facing, are thrown out and down into the "5" position. *Also* NONE.

NOT YET *phrase*. (Hanging back.) The "5" hand and forearm, hanging loosely and straight down from the elbow, move back and forth under the armpit. *Also* LATE.

NOW (nou), *adv*. (Something right in front of you.) The upturned right-angle hands drop down rather sharply. The "Y" hands may also be used.

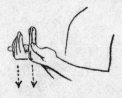

OCCASIONAL (ə kā′ zhən əl), *adj.* (The "1" finger is brought up very slowly.) The right index finger, resting in the open left palm, which is facing right, swings up slowly from its position to one in which it is pointing straight up. The movement is repeated slowly, after a pause.

ODD (ŏd), *adj.* (Something which distorts the vision.) The "C" hand describes a small arc in front of the face. *Also* CURIOUS.

OFFER (ôf′ ər), *v.*, -FERED, -FERING. (An offering; a presenting.) Both hands, slightly cupped, palms up, are held close to the chest. They move up and out in unison, describing a very slight arc. *Also* SUGGEST.

OFTEN (ôf′ ən, ŏf′ ən), *adv.* The left hand, open in the "5" position, palm up, is held before the chest. The right hand, in the right-angle position, fingers pointing up, arches over and into the left palm. This is repeated several times. *Also* FREQUENT.

OLD (ōld), *adj.* (The beard of an old man.) The right hand grasps an imaginary beard at the chin and pulls it downward.

ON (ŏn, ôn), *prep.* (Placing one hand on the other.) The right hand is placed on the back of the downturned left hand.

OPEN (ō′ pən), *adj., v.,* OPENED, OPENING. (The natural sign.) The "B" hands, palms out, are held with index finger edges touching. They swing apart so that the palms now face each other.

OPPONENT (ə pō′ nənt), *n.* (At sword's point.) The two index fingers, after pointing to each other, are drawn sharply apart. This is followed by the sign for INDIVIDUAL: Both open hands, palms facing each other, move down the sides of the body, tracing its outline to the hips. *Also* ENEMY.

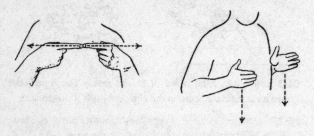

OPPOSE (ə′ pōz), *v.*, OPPOSED, OPPOSING. (Opposed to; restraint.) The tips of the right fingers, held together, are thrust purposefully into the open left palm, whose fingers are also together and pointing forward. *Also* AGAINST.

ORANGE (ôr′ ĭnj, ŏr′-), *n., adj.* (The action of squeezing an orange to get its juice into the mouth.) The right "C" hand is held at the mouth. It opens and closes deliberately, as if squeezing an orange.

ORGANIZATION (ôr′ gən ə zā′ shən), *n.* (A grouping together.) Both "C" hands, palms facing, are held a few inches apart at chest height. They are swung around in unison, so that the palms now face the body. *Also* CLASS.

OTHER (ŭŧħ′ ər), *adj.* (Moving over to another position.) The right "A" hand, thumb up, is pivoted from the wrist and swung over to the right, so that the thumb now points to the right.

OUR (our), *pron.* (An encompassing, including oneself and others.) The right hand, palm facing left, is placed at the right shoulder. It swings around to the left shoulder, its palm now facing right.

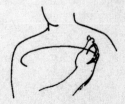

OWE (ō), *v*., OWED, OWING. (Pointing where the money should be placed.) The index finger of one hand is thrust into the upturned palm of the other several times.

P

PAIN (păn), *n*. (A stabbing pain.) The "D" hands, index fingers pointing to each other, are rotated in elliptical fashion before the chest—simultaneously but in opposite directions. *Also* HARM, HURT, INJURE.

PANTS (pănts), *n. pl.* (The natural sign.) The open hands are drawn up along the thighs, starting at the knees.

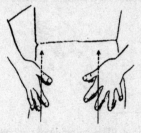

PAPER (pā′ pər), *n*. (The action of the press.) The right "5" hand, held palm down, fingers pointing left, is brought down twice against the upturned left "5" hand, whose fingers point right.

PARENTS (pâr′ əntz), *n.* (Mother and father.) Using the right "5" hand, the right thumbtip first touches the right side of the chin, then moves up to touch the right temple.

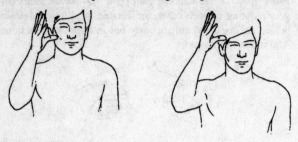

PART (pärt), *n.*, *adj.* (Cutting off or designating a part.) The little finger edge of the open right hand moves straight down the middle of the upturned left palm. *Also* SOME.

PARTY (pär′ tĭ), *n.* (The swinging of tambourines.) Both open hands, held somewhat above the head, are pivoted back and forth repeatedly, as if swinging a pair of tambourines.

PASS (păs), *v.*, PASSED, PASSING. (One hand passes the other.) Both "A" hands, palms facing each other, are held before the body, the right behind the left. The right hand moves forward, its knuckles brushing those of the left, and continues forward a bit beyond the left.

PAST (păst), *adj., n., adv.* (Something past, behind.) The upraised right hand, in the "5" position with palm facing the body, is held just above the right shoulder and is thrown back over it.

PAY (pā), *v.*, PAID, PAYING. (Giving forth of money.) The right index finger, resting in the upturned left palm, swings forward and up a bit.

PAY ATTENTION (TO) *v. phrase.* (Directing one's attention forward; applying oneself; concentrating.) Both hands, fingers pointing up and together, are held at the sides of the face. They move straight out from the face.

PEACE (pēs), *n.* (The hands are clasped as a gesture of harmony or *peace*; the opening signifies quiet or calmness.) The hands are clasped both ways, and then open and separate, assuming the "5" position, palms down.

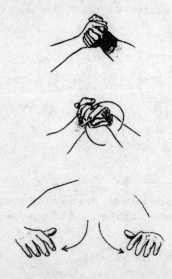

PEOPLE (pē′ pəl), *n. pl.* (The letter "P" in continuous motion, to indicate plurality.) The "P" hands, side by side, are moved alternately toward the body in continuous counterclockwise circles.

PERMANENT (pûr′ mə nənt), *adj.* (Steady, uninterrupted movement.) The "A" hands are held with palms out, thumbs extended and touching, the right behind the left. In this position the hands move forward in a straight, steady line. *Also* CONTINUE, REMAIN.

PERMISSION (pər mǐsh′ ən), *n.* (A permissive upswinging of the hands, as if giving in.) Both hands, palms facing and fingers pointing away from the body, are held at chest level, almost a foot apart. With an upward movement, using their wrists as pivots, the hands sweep up until the fingers point almost straight up. *Also* ALLOW, MAY.

PERSON (pûr′ sən), *n.* (The letter "P"; an individual is indicated.) The "P" hands, side by side, move straight down a short distance, as if outlining the sides of an unseen individual.

"PERSON" ENDING Both open hands, palms facing each other, move down the sides of the body, tracing its outline to the hips. *Also* INDIVIDUAL.

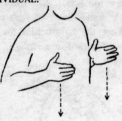

PERSUADE (pər swād′), *v.,* -SUADED, -SUADING. (Shaking someone, to implant one's will into another.) Both "A" hands, palms facing, are held before the chest, the left slightly in front of the right. In this position the hands move back and forth a short distance.

PHONE (fōn), *n., v.,* PHONED, PHONING. (The natural sign.) The right "Y" hand is placed at the right side of the head with the thumb touching the ear and the little finger touching the lips. This is the more modern telephone receiver. *Also* TELE-PHONE.

PHOTOGRAPH (fō' tə grăf´), *n.*, *v.*, -GRAPHED, -GRAPHING. (Recording an image.) The right "C" hand is held in front of the face, with thumb edge near the face and palm facing left. The hand is then brought sharply around in front of the open left hand and is struck firmly against the left palm, which is held facing forward with fingers pointing up.

 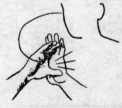

PICK (pĭk), *v.*, PICKED, PICKING. (The natural motion of selecting something from the hand.) The thumb and index fingers of the outstretched right hand grasp an imaginary object on the upturned left palm. The right hand then moves straight up. *Also* FIND.

PIE (pī), *n.* (Slicing a wedge-shaped piece of pie.) The upturned left hand represents the pie. The little finger edge of the open right hand goes through the motions of slicing a wedge-shaped piece from the pie.

PIG (pĭg), *n.* (The snout digs into the trough.) The downturned right prone hand is placed under the chin, fingers pointing forward. The hand, in this position, swings alternately up and down.

PIZZA 3, *n.* (The double "Z" in the spelling.) The curved index and middle fingers draw a "Z" in the air.

PLACE (plās), *n.* (The letter "P"; a circle or square is indicated, to show the locale or place.) The "P" hands are held side by side before the body, with middle fingertips touching. From this position, the hands separate and outline a circle (or a square), before coming together again closer to the body. *Also* POSITION.

PLAY (plā), *v.*, PLAYED, PLAYING. (Shaking tambourines.) The "Y" hands, held aloft, are shaken back and forth, pivoted at the wrists.

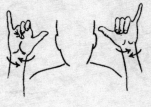

POISON (poi′ zən), *n.* (The crossed bones.) Both "S" hands are crossed and held against the chest. The signer bares the teeth, in imitation of a skull.

POLITE (pə lĭt'), *adj.* (The ruffled shirt front of a gentleman of old.) The thumb of the right "5" hand is thrust into the chest. The hand then pivots down, with thumb remaining in place. This latter part of the sign, however, is optional.

POOR (pŏŏr), *adj.* (Ragged elbows.) The open right hand is placed at the left elbow. It moves down and off, closing into the "O" position.

POPCORN (pop' kôrn), *n.* (The popping.) The index fingers alternately flick up.

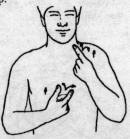

POPULATION (pop yə lā′ shən), *n*. (Running through many individuals.) The left "5" hand is held palm facing the body. The right "P" hand sweeps over the outstretched left fingers, starting at the little finger.

POP UP (*colloq.*), *v*. (Popping up before the eyes.) The right index finger, pointing up, pops up between the index and middle fingers of the left hand, whose palm faces down.

POSITION (pə zĭsh′ ən), *n*. (The letter "P"; a circle or square is indicated, to show the locale or place.) The "P" hands are held side by side before the body, with middle fingertips touching. From this position, the hands separate and outline a circle (or a square), before coming together again closer to the body. *Also* PLACE.

POWER *n.* (The curve of the flexed biceps is indicated.) The left hand, clenched into a fist, is held up, palm facing the body. The index finger of the right "D" hand moves in an arc over the left biceps muscle, from shoulder to crook of the elbow.

PRACTICE (prăk′ tĭs), *n., v.,* -TICED, -TICING. (Polishing or sharpening up.) The knuckles of the downturned right "A" hand are rubbed briskly back and forth over the side of the hand and index finger of the left "D" hand.

PRECISE (prĭ sīs′), *adj.* (The fingers come together precisely.) The thumb and index finger of each hand, palms facing, the right above the left, form circles. They are brought together with a deliberate movement, so that the fingers and thumbs now touch. Sometimes the right hand, before coming together with the left, executes a slow clockwise circle above the left.

PREGNANT (preg′ nənt), *adj.* One or both open hands are placed on the stomach and move forward an inch or two, to indicate the swollen belly.

PRESIDENT (prĕz′ ə dənt), *n.* The "C" hands, held palms out at either temple, are drawn out and up from the head into the "S" position.

PRIDE (prīd), *n., v.,* PRIDED, PRIDING. (The feelings rise up.) The thumb of the right "A" hand, palm down, moves up along the right side of the chest. A haughty expression is assumed.

PRINCIPLE (prĭn' sə pəl), *n*. (A collection or listing is indicated by the open palm, representing a page.) The right "P" hand is placed against the upper part of the open left hand, which faces right, fingers pointing upward. The right "P" hand swings down to the lower part of the left palm.

PRINT (prĭnt), *v*., PRINTED, PRINTING. (The act of printing block letters.) The right index finger traces letters in the upturned left palm.

PRIVACY (prī' və sĭ), *n*. (The sealing of the lips; keeping the words back.) The back of the thumb of the right "A" hand is placed firmly against the closed lips. The thumb, in this position, may move off the lips slightly and return again to the lips. As an optional addition, the thumb may swing down under the downturned cupped left hand, after being placed on the lips as above.

PROCEED (prə sēd'), v., -CEEDED, -CEEDING. (Moving forward.) Both right-angle hands, palms facing each other and knuckles facing forward, move forward simultaneously.

PROGRAM (prō' grăm, -grəm), n. (The letter "P"; a listing on both sides of the page.) The thumb side of the right "P" hand is placed against the palm of the open left hand, which is facing right. The right "P" hand moves down the left palm. The left hand then swings around so that its palm faces the body. The right "P" hand then moves over and down the back of the left hand.

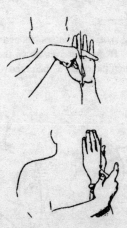

PROGRESS (*n.* prŏg′ rĕs; *v.* prə grĕs′), -GRESSED, -GRESSING. (Moving forward, step by step.) Both hands, in the right angle position, palms facing, are held before the chest, a few inches apart, with the right hand slightly behind the left. The right hand is brought up, over and forward, so that it is now ahead of the left. The left hand then follows suit, so that it is now ahead of the right.

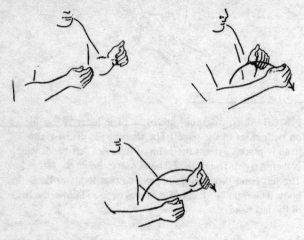

PROJECT (proj′ ekt), *n.* (The letters "P" and "J.") The middle finger of the right "P" hand moves down the left palm, held facing the body. Then the right "J" hand moves down the back of the left hand.

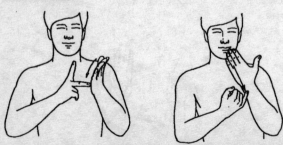

PROMISE (prŏm′ ĭs), *n., v.,* -ISED, -ISING. (The arm is raised.) The right index finger is placed at the lips. The right arm is then raised, palm out and elbow resting on the back of the left hand. *Also* SWEAR.

PROMOTE (prə mōt′), *v.,* -MOTED, -MOTING. (Something high up.) Both hands, in the right angle position, are held before the face, about a foot apart, palms facing. They are raised abruptly about a foot, in a slight outward curving movement.

PROOF (pro͞of), *n.* (Laying out the proof for all to see.) The back of the open right hand is placed with a flourish on the open left palm. The index finger may first touch the lips.

PROTECT (prə tĕkt′), *v.,* -TECTED, -TECTING. (Hold down firmly; cover and strengthen.) The "S" hands, downturned, are held side by side in front of the body, the arms almost horizontal, and the left hand in front of the right. Both arms move a short distance forward and slightly downward.

PROVIDE (prə vīd′), *v.,* -VIDED, -VIDING. (Handing over.) The "AND" hands are held upright with palms toward the body. From this position they swing forward and down, opening up as if giving something out.

PUNISH (pŭn' ĭsh), *v.*, -ISHED, -ISHING. (A striking movement.) The right index finger strikes the left elbow with a glancing blow.

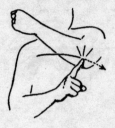

PURPOSE (pûr' pəs), *n.* (Relative standing of one's thoughts.) A modified sign for THINK is made: The right index finger touches the middle of the forehead. The tips of the right "V" hand, palm down, are then thrust into the upturned left palm (as in STAND, *q.v.*). The right "V" hand is then rethrust into the upturned left palm, with right palm now facing the body.

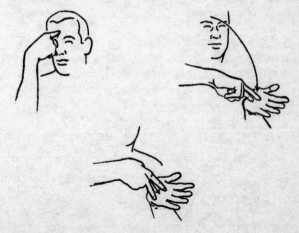

PUT (po͝ot), *v.*, PUT, PUTTING. (Moving from one place to another.) The downturned hands, fingers touching their respective thumbs, move in unison from left to right. *Also* MOVE.

QUARREL (kwôr′ əl, kwŏr′-), *n.*, *v.* -RELED, -RELING.
(Repeated rejoinders.) Both "D" hands are held with index fingers pointing toward each other. The hands move up and down alternately, each pivoting in turn at the wrist.

QUESTION (kwĕs′ chən), *n.* (The natural sign.) The right index finger draws a question mark in the air.

QUIT (kwĭt), *v.*, QUIT, QUITTING. (Pulling out.) The index and middle fingers of the right "H" hand are grasped by the left hand. The right hand pulls out of the left.

QUOTATION (kwō tā′ shən), *n*. (The quotation marks are indicated.) The curved index and middle fingers of both hands, held palms out, move slightly to either side of the body, as if drawing quotation marks in the air.

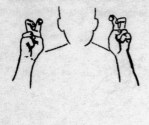

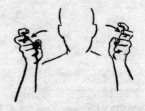

R

RACE (rās), *n., v.,* RACED, RACING. (Opposing objects.) The "A" hands are held side by side before the chest, palms facing each other and thumbs pointing forward. In this position the hands move alternately back and forth, toward and away from the body. *Also* COMPETE.

RAILROAD (rāl' rōd'), *n.* (The letter "R".) The right "R" hand, palm down, moves down an inch or two, and moves to the right in a small arc.

RAINBOW (rān' bō), *n.* (Tracing the colors across the sky.) The right "4" hand, palm facing the signer, describes an arc in the air, from left to right.

RAISE (rāz), *n., v.,* RAISED, RAISING. (Adding on.) The index and middle fingers of the right "H" hand, palm up, are swung up and over until they come to rest on the index and middle fingers of the left "H" hand, held palm down. *Also* ADD.

READ (rēd), *v.,* READ, READING. (The eyes scan the page.) The left hand is held before the body, palm up and fingers pointing to the right. This represents the page. The right "V" hand then moves down as if scanning the page.

READY *adj., adv.* (The "R" hands.) With palms facing down, both "R" hands move simultaneously from left to right.

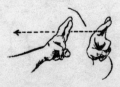

REAL (rē′ əl, rēl), *adj.* (Coming forth directly from the lips; true.) The index finger of the right "D" hand, palm facing left, is placed against the lips. It moves up an inch or two and then describes a small arc forward and away from the lips.

REASON (rē′ zən), *n.* (The letter "R"; the thought.) The fingertips of the right "R" hand describe a small counterclockwise circle in the middle of the forehead.

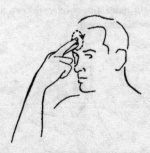

RECENT (rē′ sənt), *adj.* (The slight movement represents a slight amount of time.) With the closed right hand held with knuckles against the right cheek, the thumbtip flicks off the tip of the curved index finger a number of times. The eyes squint a bit and the lips are drawn out in a slight smile. The hand remains against the cheek during the flicking movement. Sometimes, instead of the flicking movement, the tip of the curved index finger scratches slightly up and down against the cheek. In this case, the palm faces back toward the shoulder. The same expression is used as in the flicking movement.

RED (rĕd), *adj., n.* (The lips, which are red, are indicated.) The tip of the right index finger moves down across the lips. The "R" hand may also be used.

REDUCE (ri dūs′, -dōōs′), *v.*, -DUCED, -DUCING. (The diminishing size or amount.) With palms facing, the right hand is

held above the left. The right hand moves slowly down toward
the left, but does not touch it.

REFUSE (rǐ fūz′), *v.*, -FUSED, -FUSING. (Holding back.) The
right "A" hand, palm facing left, moves up sharply to a position above the right shoulder.

REGRET (rǐ grĕt′), *n.*, *v.*, -GRETTED, -GRETTING. (The heart is
circled, to indicate feeling, modified by the letter "S," for
SORRY.) The right "S" hand, palm facing the body, is rotated
several times over the area of the heart. *Also* SORROW.

REGULAR (rĕg′ yə lər), *adj.* (Coming together with regular frequency.) Both "D" hands are held with index fingers pointing forward, the right hand above the left. The right "D" hand is brought down on the left several times in rhythmic succession as both hands move forward.

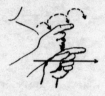

RELY (rĭ lī′), *v.*, -LIED, -LYING. (Hanging on to.) With the right index finger resting across its left counterpart, both hands drop down a bit.

REMAIN (rĭ mān′), *v.*, -MAINED, -MAINING. (Steady, uninterrupted movement.) The "A" hands are held with palms out, thumbs extended and touching, the right behind the left. In this position the hands move forward in a straight, steady line. *Also* CONTINUE, PERMANENT.

REMAINDER (rĭ măn′ dər), *n.* (The remainder is left behind.) The "5" hands, palms facing each other and fingers pointing forward, are dropped simultaneously a few inches, as if dropping something on the table.

REMEMBER (rĭ měm′ bər), *v.*, -BERED, -BERING. (Knowledge which remains.) The sign for KNOW is made: The right fingertips are placed on the forehead. The sign for REMAIN then follows: The "A" hands are held with palms toward the body, thumbs extended and touching, the right behind the left. In this position the hands move forward in a straight, steady line, or straight down.

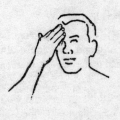

REMOVE (rĭ mōōv′), *v.*, -MOVED, -MOVING. (Removing.) The right "A" hand, resting in the palm of the left "5" hand, moves slightly up and away, describing a small arc. It is then cast downward, opening into the "5" position, palm down, as if removing something from the left hand and casting it down.

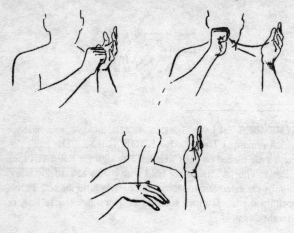

REPLACE (rĭ plās′), *v.*, -PLACED, -PLACING. (Exchanging places.) The right "A" hand, positioned above the left "A" hand, swings down and under the left, coming up a bit in front of it. *Also* EXCHANGE.

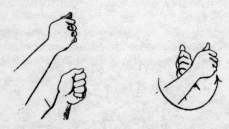

REQUIRE (rĭ kwīr′), *v.*, -QUIRED, -QUIRING. (Something specific is moved in toward oneself.) The palm of the left "5" hand faces right. The right index finger is thrust into the left palm, and both hands are drawn sharply in toward the chest.

RESERVATION (rĕz´ ər vā´ shən), *n*. (Binding the hands down.) The downturned, right "S" hand makes a single, clockwise circle and comes down to rest on the back of the downturned, left "S" hand. *Also* APPOINTMENT.

RESPECT (rĭ spĕkt´), *n., v.,* -SPECTED, -SPECTING. (The letter "R"; bowing the head.) The right "R" hand swings up in an arc toward the head, which bows somewhat as the hand moves up toward it. The hand's movement is sometimes reversed, moving down and away from the head in an arc, while the head bows.

RESPONSIBILITY (rĭ spŏn´ sə bĭl´ ə tĭ), *n.* (Something which weighs down or burdens one with responsibility.) The fingertips of both hands, placed on the right shoulder, bear down.

REST (rĕst), *n.* (The folded arms; a position of rest.) With palms facing the body, the arms are folded across the chest.

RESTRICT (rĭ strĭkt´), *v.,* -STRICTED, -STRICTING. (The upper and lower limits are defined.) The right-angle hands, palms facing, are held before the body, the right above the left. They swing out 45 degrees simultaneously, pivoted from their wrists.

REVENGE (rĭ vĕnj′), *n., v.,* -VENGED, -VENGING. (Birds pecking back and forth at each other.) The right index finger and thumb, pressed together, strike their left counterparts with force.

REVOLUTION (rev ə lo͞o′ shən), *n.* (The letter "R"; a whirlwind.) Both "R" hands, fingertips pointing at each other, are held with the right above the left. The "R" fingers spin around each other in a sudden and dramatic movement.

RHINOCEROS (rī nos′ ər əs), *n.* (The horn.) The right "I" hand, palm facing left and thumb tucked under the fingers, is placed on the nose. The hand moves forward and up in an arc, tracing the characteristic shape of the horn.

RIGHT (rīt), *adj., adv.* The right index finger, held above the left index finger, comes down rather forcefully so that the bottom of the right hand comes to rest on top of the left thumb joint. *Also* CORRECT.

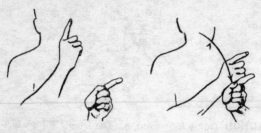

ROAD (rōd), *n.* (The winding movement.) Both hands, palms facing and fingers together and extended straight out, move in unison away from the body, in a winding manner.

ROOM (rōom, rŏom), *n.* (The dimensions are indicated.) The open hands, palms facing and fingers pointing out, are dropped an inch or two simultaneously. They then shift their relative positions so that both palms face the body, with one hand in front of the other. In this new position they again drop an inch or two simultaneously.

ROOMY (rōō′ mē), *adj.* (Lots of elbow room.) The "S" hands, palms facing, are positioned at chest height. As the elbows move apart the palms move down.

ROUGH (rŭf), *adj.* (The "roughness," in the form of ridges, described.) The tips of the curved right fingers trace imaginary ridges over the upright left palm, from the base of the hand to the fingertips. The action is repeated several times.

RULE (rōōl), *n., v.,* RULED, RULING. (Holding the reins over all.) The "A" hands, palms facing, move alternately back and forth, as if grasping and manipulating reins. The left "A" hand, still in position, swings over so that its palm now faces down. The right hand opens to the "5" position, palm down, and swings over the left, which moves slightly to the right.

RUN (rŭn), *v.*, RAN, RUN, RUNNING. The open left hand is held pointing out, palm down. The open right hand is held beneath it, facing up. The right hand is thrown forward rather quickly so the palm brushes repeatedly across the palm of the left.

RUN AWAY *v. phrase.* (Slipping out and away.) The right index finger is held pointing upward between the index and middle fingers of the prone left hand. From this position the right index finger moves to the right, slipping out of the grasp of the left fingers and away from the left hand.

S

SAD (săd), *adj.* (The facial features drop.) Both "5" hands, palms facing the eyes and fingers slightly curved, drop simultaneously to a level with the mouth. The head drops slightly as the hands move down, and an expression of sadness is assumed.

SAID (sĕd), *v.* (Words tumbling from the mouth.) The right index finger, pointing left, describes a continuous small circle in front of the mouth. *Also* HEARING, SAY, SPEECH.

SALARY (săl′ ə rĭ), *n.* (EARN, MONEY.) The sign for EARN is made: the right "5" hand, its little finger edge resting on the upturned left palm, moves toward the left and closes into the "S" position. This is followed by MONEY: The upturned right fingertips, grasping a wad of imaginary dollar bills, slaps down on the left palm.

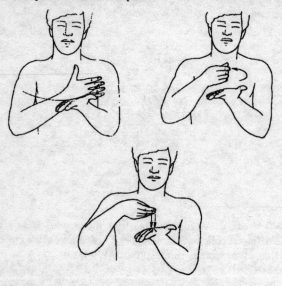

SALE (sāl), *n.* (Transferring ownership of an object.) Both "AND" hands, fingers touching their respective thumbs, are held palms down before the body. The hands are pivoted simultaneously outward and away from the body, once or several times.

SALT (sôlt), *n*. (The act of tapping the salt from a knife edge.) Both "H" hands, palms down, are held before the chest. The fingers of the right "H" hand tap those of the left several times.

SAME (săm), *adj*. (Matching fingers are brought together.) The outstretched index fingers are brought together, either once or several times.

SANDWICH (sănd' wĭch, săn'-), *n*. (In between slices.) The fingers of the upturned right hand are tucked between the middle and third fingers of the left hand, whose palm faces the signer. The motion may be repeated.

SATISFACTION (săt´ ĭs făk´ shən), *n.* (The inner feelings settle down.) Both "B" hands (or "5" hands, fingers together) are placed palms down against the chest, the right above the left. Both move down simultaneously a few inches.

SAY (sā), *v.,* SAID, SAYING. (Words tumbling from the mouth.) The right index finger, pointing left, describes a continuous small circle in front of the mouth. *Also* HEARING, SAID, SPEAK.

SCHOOL (sko͞ol), *n.* (The teachers hands are clapped for attention.) The hands are clapped together several times.

SCIENCE (sī´ əns), *n.* (Pouring alternately from test tubes.) The upright thumbs of both "A" hands swing over alternately in elliptical fashion, as if pouring out the contents of a pair of test tubes.

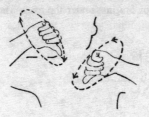

SCREAM (skrēm), *v.*, SCREAMED, SCREAMING. (Harsh words thrown out.) The right hand, as in CURSE 1, appears to claw words out of the mouth. This time, however, it turns and throws them out, ending in the "5" position.

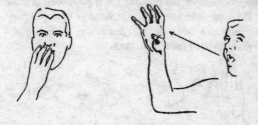

SCREW (skrōō), *n., v.* (The movement.) The right index finger makes a clockwise turn in the left palm.

SEE (sē), *v.*, SAW, SEEN, SEEING. (The eyesight is directed forward.) The right "V" hand, palm facing the body, is placed so that the fingertips are just under the eyes. The hand swings straight out.

SEEM (sēm), *v.*, SEEMED, SEEMING. (Something presented before the eyes.) The open right hand, palm flat and facing out, with fingers together and pointing up, is positioned at shoulder level. Pivoting from the wrist, the hand is swung around so that the palm now faces the eyes. Sometimes the eyes glance at the newly presented palm. *Also* LOOK.

SELFISH (sĕl′ fĭsh), *adj.* (Pulling things toward oneself.) Both prone open or "V" hands are held in front of the body with fingers bent. The hands are then drawn quickly and forcefully inward, as if raking things toward oneself.

SEND (sĕnd), *v.*, SENT, SENDING. (Sending away from.) The right fingertips tap the back of the downturned, left "S" hand and then swing forward, away from the hand.

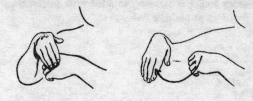

SENSITIVE (sĕn′ sə tĭv), *adj.* (A nimble touch.) The middle finger of the right hand touches the chest over the heart very briefly and lightly, and is then flicked off.

SEPARATE (sĕp′ ə rāt′),*v.*, *adj.*, *n.* (Separating to classify.) Both hands, in the right angle position, are placed palms down before the body, knuckles to knuckles. They pull apart or separate, once or a number of times.

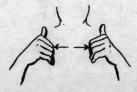

SEVERAL (sĕv′ ər əl), *adj.* (The fingers are presented in order, to convey the concept of "several.") The right "A" hand is held palm facing up. One by one the fingers open, beginning with the index finger and ending with the little finger. Some use only the index and middle fingers.

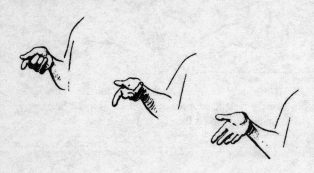

SEWING MACHINE *n.* (The needle moves over the cloth.) The left index finger points straight forward. The right thumb and index, forming a somewhat elongated circle, moves forward repeatedly over the left index, from knuckle to tip, imitating the up-down movement of the needle.

SHE (shē), *pron.* (Pointing at a female.) The FEMALE prefix sign is made: The right "A" hand's thumb moves down along the line of the right jaw, from ear almost to chin. The right index finger then points at an imaginary female. If in context the gender is clear, the prefix sign is usually omitted. *Also* HER.

SHINE (shīn), *v.*, SHINED, SHINING, SHONE. (Reflected glistening of light rays.) The left hand, held supinely before the chest, palm down, represents the object from which the rays glisten. The right hand, in the "5" position, touches the back of the left lightly and moves up toward the right, pivoting slightly at the wrist, with fingers wiggling.

SHOCKED (shŏkt), *adj.*, *v.* (The mind is frozen; the thought is frozen.) The index finger of the right "D" hand, palm facing the body, touches the forehead (modified THINK sign, *q.v.*). Both hands, in the "5" position, palms down, are then suddenly and deliberately dropped down in front of the body. A look of surprise is assumed at this point, and the head jerks back slightly.

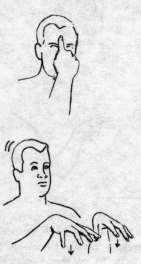

SHOP (shŏp), *n.*, *v.*, SHOPPED, SHOPPING. (Paying out money.) The right hand, palm up and all fingertips touching the thumb, is placed in the upturned left hand. From this position it moves forward and off the left hand a number of times. The right fingers usually remain against the thumb, but they may be opened very slightly each time the right hand moves forward.

SHORT (shôrt), *adj.* (To make short; to measure off a short space.) The index and middle fingers of the right "H" hand are placed across the top of the index and middle fingers of the left "H" hand, and move a short distance back and forth, along the length of the left index finger.

SICK (sĭk), *adj., adv.* (The sick parts of the anatomy are indicated.) The right middle finger rests on the forehead, and its left counterpart is placed against the stomach. The signer assumes an expression of sadness or physical distress. *Also* ILL.

SIGHT (sīt), *n.,* SAW, SEEN, SEEING. (The eyesight is directed forward.) The right "V" hand, palm facing the body, is placed so that the fingertips are just under the eyes. The hand swings straight out. *Also* SEE.

SIGN LANGUAGE *n.* (LANGUAGE, *q.v.*, and hand/arm movements.) The "D" hands, palms facing and index fingers pointing back toward the face, describe a series of continuous counterclockwise circles toward and away from the face, imitating the foot motions in bicycling. This is followed by the sign for LANGUAGE: The downturned "F" or "L" hands are positioned with thumbs and index fingertips touching. The hands move straight apart to either side in a wavy motion. The LANGUAGE part is often omitted.

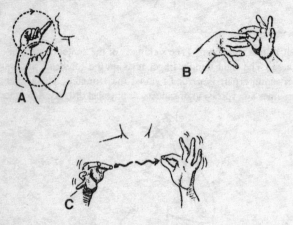

SISTER (sĭs′ tər), *n.* (Female root sign: SAME. Meaning a female from the same family.) The FEMALE root sign is made: The thumb of the right "A" hand moves down along the right jawbone, almost to the chin. This is followed by the sign for SAME: The outstretched index fingers are brought together, either once or several times.

SKI (skē), *v.* (The ski poles.) The signer, holding an imaginary pair of ski poles, pushes down on them in order to create forward motion.

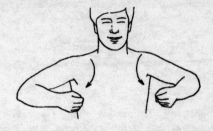

SKILL (skĭl), *n.* (A sharp-edged hand.) The right hand grasps the little finger edge of the left firmly. As it leaves this position, moving down and out, it assumes the "A" position, palm facing left.

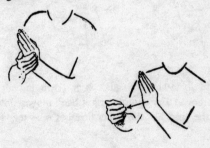

SLEEP (slēp) *n., v.* (The natural sign.) The signer's head leans to the right and rests in the upturned palm of the open right hand.

SLOW (slō), *adj.* (The movement indicates the slowness.) The right hand is drawn slowly over the back of the downturned left hand, from fingertips to wrist.

SMART (smärt), *adj.* (The mind is bright.) The middle finger is placed at the forehead, and then the hand, with an outward flick, turns around so that the palm faces outward. This indicates a brightness flowing from the mind. *Also* INTELLIGENT.

SMELL (smĕl), *v.*, SMELLED, SMELLING, *n.* (Bringing something up to the nose.) The upturned right hand moves slowly up to and past the nose, and the signer breathes in as the hand sweeps by.

SMILE (smīl), *v.*, SMILED, SMILING, *n.* (Drawing the lips into a smile.) The right index finger is drawn back over the lips,

toward the ear. As the finger moves back, the signer breaks
into a smile. (Both index fingers may also be used.)

SNEEZE (snēz), *v., n.* (Stifling a sneeze.) The index finger is
pressed lengthwise under the nose.

SNOB (snob), *n.* (The upturned nose.) The right thumb and
index finger, slightly open, are placed at the tip of the nose,
and move up, coming together as they do.

SOCIAL SECURITY *n.* (The "S" letters.) The signer finger-spells the letters "S-S."

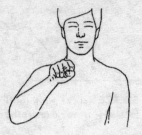

SODA POP *n.* (Corking a bottle.) The left "O" hand is held with thumb edge up, representing a bottle. The thumb and index finger of the right "5" hand represent a cork, and are inserted into the circle formed by the "O" hand. The palm of the open right hand then strikes down on the upturned edge of the "O" hand, as if forcing the cork into the bottle.

SOME (sŭm; *unstressed* səm), *adj.* (Cutting off or designating a part.) The little finger edge of the open right hand moves straight down the middle of the upturned left palm. *Also* PART.

SON (sŭn), *n.* (Male, baby.) The sign for MALE is made: The thumb and extended fingers of the right hand are brought up to grasp an imaginary cap brim. This is followed by the sign for BABY: The arms are held with one resting on the other, as if cradling a baby.

SORROW (sŏr′ ō, sôr′ ō), *n.* (The heart is circled, to indicate feeling, modified by the letter "S," for SORRY.) The right "S" hand, palm facing the body, is rotated several times over the area of the heart. *Also* REGRET.

SPEAK (spĕk), *v.*, SPOKE, SPOKEN, SPEAKING. (Words tumbling from the mouth.) The right index finger, pointing left, describes a continuous small circle in front of the mouth. *Also* HEARING, SAID, SAY, SPEECH.

SPECIAL (spĕsh′ əl), *adj.* (Selecting a particular item from among several.) The index finger and thumb of the right hand grasp and pull up the left index finger.

SPEECH (spēch), *n.* (A gesture of an orator.) The right open hand, palm facing left, is held above and to the right of the head. It pivots, forward and backward, on the wrist several times.

SPEECHLESS (spēch' lĭs), *(colloq.)*, *adj.* (The mouth drops open.) The fingertips of both "V" hands are held curved and touching before the body, one hand above the other. Then the hands are suddenly drawn apart, and at the same instant the mouth drops open and the eyes open wide.

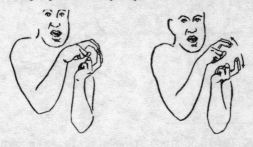

SPORTS (spôrtz), *n.* (A challenge.) Both hands are held in the "A" position, knuckles facing and thumbs standing up. They come together forcefully.

SPRING (sprĭng), *n.* (Flowers or plants emerge from the ground.) The right fingers, pointing up, emerge from the closed left hand, and they spread open as they do. The action may be repeated. *Also* GROW.

STAMP (stămp), *n*. (Licking the stamp.) The tips of the right index and middle fingers are licked with the tongue, and then the fingers are pressed against the upturned left palm, as if affixing a stamp to an envelope.

STAND (stănd), *v*., STOOD, STANDING, *n*. (The feet planted on the ground.) The downturned right "V" fingers are thrust into the upturned left palm.

STANDARD (stan′ dərd), *adj.*, *n*. (The same all around.) Both downturned "Y" hands execute counterclockwise circles.

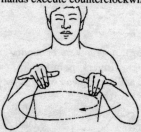

STATISTICS (stə tis′ tiks), *n.* (The letter "S"; the multiplication symbol.) Both "S" hands repeatedly cross each other as in the "X" symbol for multiplication.

STEAL (stēl), *n., v.,* STOLE, STOLEN, STEALING. (The hand, partly concealed, takes something surreptitiously.) The index and middle fingers of the right hand, somewhat curved, are placed under the left elbow. As they move slowly along the left forearm toward the left wrist, they close a bit.

STILL (stĭl), *adv., conj.* (Duration of movement from past to present.) The right "Y" hand is held palm down in front of the right shoulder and is then moved slowly down and forward in a smooth curve.

STOP (stŏp), *v.*, STOPPED, STOPPING, *n.* (A stopping or cutting short.) The little finger edge of the right hand is thrust abruptly into the upturned left palm, indicating a cutting short.

STORY (stôr′ ĭ), *n.* (The unraveling or stretching out of words or sentences.) Both open hands are held close to each other, with fingers open and palms facing and almost touching. As the hands are drawn apart, the thumb and index finger of each hand come together to form circles. This is repeated several times.

STUBBORN (stŭb′ ərn), *adj.* (The donkey's broad ear; the animal is traditionally a stubborn one.) The open hand, or the "B" hand, is placed at the side of the head, with palm out and fingers pointing straight up. The hand moves forward and back, pivoting at the wrist, as in the case of a donkey's ears flapping. Both hands may also be used, at either side of the head.

STUCK (stŭk), *adj.* (Impaled on a stick, as a snake's head.) The "V" fingers are thrust into the throat.

STUDENT (stū′ dənt, stōō′-), *n.* (One who learns.) The sign for LEARN is made: The downturned fingers of the right hand are placed on the upturned left palm. They close, and then the hand rises and the right fingertips are placed on the forehead. This is followed by the sign for INDIVIDUAL: Both open hands, palms facing each other, move down the sides of the body, tracing its outline to the hips.

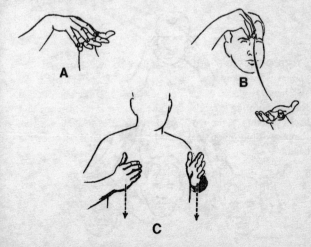

STUPID (stū' pĭd, stōō'-), *adj.* (Knocking the head to indicate its empty state.) The "S" hand, palm facing the body, knocks against the forehead.

SUCCEED (sək sēd'), *v.*, -CEEDED, -CEEDING. (Penetrating the heights.) The "D" hands, palms back, are held at each side of the head, near the temples. With a pivoting motion of the wrists, the hands swing up and around, simultaneously, to a position above the head, with palms facing out.

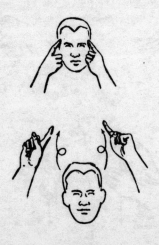

SUFFER (sŭf' ər), v., -FERED, -FERING. (A clenching of the fists; the rise and fall of pain.) Both "S" hands, tightly clenched, revolve about each other, slowly and deliberately, while a pained expression is worn.

SUGAR (shŏŏg' ər), n. (Titillating to the taste.) The fingertips of the right "U" hand, palm facing the body, brush against the chin a number of times beginning at the lips. *Also* CUTE.

SUGGEST (səg jĕst'), *v.*, -GESTED, -GESTING. (An offering; a presenting.) Both hands, slightly cupped, palms up, are held close to the chest. They move up and out in unison, describing a very slight arc. *Also* OFFER.

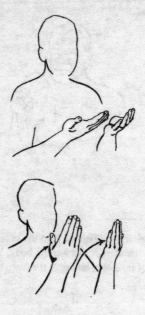

SUMMER (sŭm' ər), *n.* (Wiping the brow.) The downturned right index finger, slightly curved, is drawn across the forehead from left to right.

SUN (sŭn), *n., v.,* SUNNED, SUNNING. (The round shape and the rays.) The right index finger, pointing forward and held above the face, describes a small clockwise circle. The right hand, all fingers touching the thumb, then drops down and forward from its position above the head. As it does so, the fingers open to the "5" position.

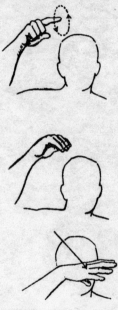

SUNRISE (sŭn′ rīz′), *n.* (The natural sign.) The downturned left arm, held horizontally, represents the horizon. The right thumb and index finger form a circle, and this circle is drawn up from a position in front of the downturned left hand.

SUNSET (sŭn′ sĕt′), *n.* (The natural sign.) The movement described in SUNRISE is reversed, with the right hand moving down below the downturned left hand.

SUPERVISE (sōō′ pər vīz′), *v.*, -VISED, -VISING. (The eyes sweep back and forth.) The "V" hands, held crossed, describe a counterclockwise circle before the chest.

SUPPORT (sə pōrt′), *n.*, *v.* -PORTED, -PORTING. (Holding up.) The right "S" hand pushes up the left "S" hand.

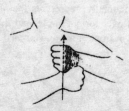

SUPPOSE (sə pōz′), *v.,* -POSED, -POSING. (To have an idea.) The little fingertip of the right "I" hand taps the right temple once or twice.

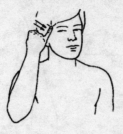

SURPRISE (sər prīz′), *v.,* -PRISED, -PRISING, *n.* (The eyes pop open in amazement.) Both hands are held in modified "O" positions with thumb and index fingers of each hand near the eyes. These fingers suddenly flick open, and the eyes simultaneously pop open wide.

SURRENDER (sə rĕn′ dər), *v.,* -DERED, -DERING. (Throwing up the hands in a gesture of surrender.) Both "A" hands are held palms down before the chest and then thrown up in unison, ending in the "5" position.

SWEAR (swâr), *v.* SWORE, SWORN, SWEARING. (The arm is raised.) The right index finger is placed at the lips. The right arm is then raised, palm out and elbow resting on the back of the left hand. *Also* PROMISE.

SWEETHEART (swēt′ härt′), *(colloq.)*, *n.* (Heads nodding toward each other.) The "A" hands are placed together before the body with thumbs up. The thumbs wiggle up and down. *Also* LOVER.

SYMPATHY (sĭm′ pə thĭ), *n.* (Feelings from the heart, conferred on others.) The middle fingertip of the open right hand touches the chest over the heart. The same open hand then moves in a small, clockwise circle before the right shoulder, with palm facing forward and fingers pointing up. *Also* MERCY.

T

TALL (tôl), *adj.* (The height is indicated.) The index finger of the right "D" hand moves straight up against the palm of the left "5" hand.

_____

TAPE RECORDER *n.* (The movement of the spools.) Both hands are held downturned, with middle fingers hanging down. Both hands move in unison, in a clockwise direction.

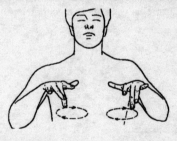

_____

TEA (tē), *n.* (Stirring the teabag.) The right hand, holding an imaginary tea bag, executes a circular, stirring motion into the left "O" hand, shaped like a cup.

TEACH (tēch), *v.*, TAUGHT, TEACHING. (Giving forth from the mind.) The fingertips of each hand are placed on the temples. They then swing out and open into the "5" position. *Also* EDUCATE, INSTRUCT.

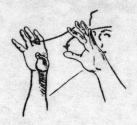

TELEPHONE (tĕl' ə fōn'), *n., v.*, -PHONED, -PHONING. (The natural sign.) The right "Y" hand is placed at the right side of the head with the thumb touching the ear and the little finger touching the lips. This is the more modern telephone receiver. *Also* PHONE.

TELL ME *phrase.* (The natural sign.) The tip of the index finger of the right "D" hand, palm facing the body, is first placed at the lips and then moves down to touch the chest.

TEMPERATURE (tĕm′ pər ə chər, -prə chər), *n.* (The rise and fall of the mercury in the thermometer.) The index finger of the right "D" hand, pointing left, moves slowly up and down the index finger of the left "D" hand, which is held pointing up.

TEMPT (tĕmpt), *v.*, TEMPTED, TEMPTING. (Tapping one surreptitiously at a concealed place.) With the left arm held palm down before the chest, the curved right index finger taps the left elbow a number of times.

TEND (tĕnd), *v.*, TENDED, TENDING. (The feelings of the heart move toward a specific object.) The tip of the right middle finger touches the heart. The open right hand, palm facing the body, then moves away from the heart toward the palm of the open left hand.

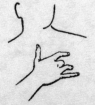 

TEST (tĕst), *n., v.,* TESTED, TESTING. (A series of questions, spread out on a page.) Both "D" hands, palms down, simultaneously execute a single circle, the right hand moving in a clockwise direction and the left in a counterclockwise direction. Upon completion of the circle, both hands open into the "5" position and move straight down a short distance. (The hands actually draw question marks in the air.)

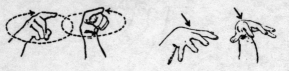

THANK YOU *phrase.* (Words extended politely from the mouth.) The fingertips of the right "5" hand are placed at the mouth. The hand moves away from the mouth to a palm-up position before the body. The signer meanwhile usually nods smilingly.

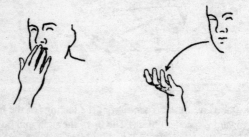

THAT (t͟hat, *unstressed* t͟hət), *pron.* (Something specific.) The downturned right "Y" hand is placed on the upturned left palm.

THEIR(S) (t͟hâr, *unstressed* t͟hər), *pron.* (Belonging to; pushed toward.) The open right hand, palm facing out and fingers together and pointing up, moves out a short distance from the body. This is repeated several times, with the hand moving an inch or two toward the right each time. The hand may also be swept in a short left-to-right arc in this position.

THEM (t͟hĕm, unstressed t͟həm), *pron.* (The natural sign.) The right index finger points in turn to a number of imaginary persons or objects.

THEMSELVES (t͟həm sĕlvz′), *pron. pl.* (The thumb indicates an individual, *i.e., a self;* several are indicated.) The right hand, in the "A" position with thumb pointing up, makes a series of short forward movements as it sweeps either from right to left, or from left to right.

THERE 1 (t͟hâr), *adv.* (The natrual sing.) The right index finger points to an imaginary object, usually at or slightly above eye level, *i.e.,* "yonder."

THIN (thĭn), *adj.* (The drawn face.) The thumb and index finger run down the cheeks, which are drawn in.

THING (thĭng), *n.* (Something shown in the hand.) The outstretched right hand, palm up and held before the chest, is dropped slightly and brought over a bit to the right.

THINK (thĭngk), *v.,* THOUGHT, THINKING. (A thought is turned over in the mind.) The index finger makes a small circle on the forehead.

THIRST (thûrst), *n.* (The parched throat.) The index finger moves down the throat a short distance.

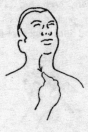

THIS MONTH *phrase.* (Now, month.) The sign for NOW is made: The upturned right-angle hands drop down rather sharply. The "Y" hands may also be used. This is followed by the sign for MONTH: The extended right index finger moves down along the upturned, extended left index finger. The two signs are sometimes given in reverse order.

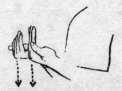 

THOUSAND (thou′ zənd), *n.* ("M" for the Latin *mille*, thousand.) The tips of the right "M" hand are thrust into the upturned left plam.

THROUGH (thrōō), *adv., prep., adj.* (The natural movement.) The open right hand is pushed between either the middle and index or the middle and third fingers of the open left hand.

TICKET (tĭk′ ĭt), *n.* (A baggage check or ticket.) The sides of the ticket are outlined with the thumb and index finger of each hand. Then the middle knuckles of the second and third fingers of the right hand squeeze the outer edge of the left palm, as a conductor's ticket punch.

TIGER (tĭ′ gər), *n.* (The stripes on the face.) The claw hands trace the cat's stripes on the face.

TILL (tĭl), *prep.* (From one point to the next.) The extended right index finger moves forward slowly and comes to rest on the tip of the extended, upturned left index finger.

TIME (tīm), *n.* (Time by the clock, indicated by the ticking of the clock or watch.) The curved right index finger taps the back of the left wrist several times.

TODAY (tə dā′), *n.* (Now, day.) The sign for NOW is made: The upturned right-angle hands drop down rather sharply. The "Y" hands may also be used. This is followed by the sign for DAY: The left arm, held horizontally, palm down, represents the horizon. The right elbow rests on the back of the left hand, with the right arm in a perpendicular position. The right "D" hand, palm facing left, moves in an arc to the left until it is just above the left elbow. The two signs may be reversed.

TOILET (toi′ lĭt), *n.* (The letter "T.") The right "T" hand is shaken slightly.

TOMORROW (tə môr′ ō, -mŏr′ ō), *n., adv.* (A single step ahead, *i.e.*, into the future.) The thumb of the right "A" hand, placed on the right cheek, moves straight out from the face, describing an arc.

TONIGHT (tə nīt′), *n.* (Now, night.) The sign for NOW is made: The upturned right-angle hands drop down rather sharply. The "Y" hands may also be used. This is followed by the sign for NIGHT: The left hand, palm down, is positioned at chest height. The downturned right hand, held an inch or so above the left, moves over the left hand in an arc, as the sun setting beneath the horizon. The two signs may be reversed.

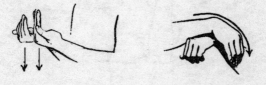

TRAIN (trān), *n.* (Running along the tracks.) The "V" hands are held palms down. The right "V" moves back and forth over the left "V."

TRAVEL (trăv′ əl), *n., v.,* -ELED, -ELING. (Moving around from place to place.) The downturned curved "V" fingers of the right hand describe a series of small counterclockwise circles as they move in random fashion from right to left.

TREE (trē), *n.* (The shape.) The elbow of the upright right arm rests on the palm of the upturned left hand. This is the trunk. The right "5" fingers wiggle to imitate the movement of the branches and leaves.

U

UNCLE (ŭng′ kəl), *n.* (The letter "U"; the "male" or upper portion of the head.) The right "U" hand is held near the right temple and is shaken slightly.

UNDER (ŭn′ dər), *prep.* (The area below.) The right "A" hand, thumb pointing up, moves in a counterclockwise fashion under the downturned left hand.

UNDERSTAND (ŭn′ dər stănd′), *v* -STOOD, -STANDING. (An awakening of the mind.) The right "S" hand is placed on the forehead, palm facing the body. The index finger suddenly flicks up into the "D" position.

237

UPSET (up set'), *adj.*, *v.* (The stomach is turned upside down.) The downturned open right hand is positioned horizontally across the stomach. It flips over so that it is now palm up.

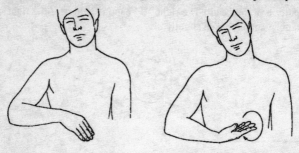

US (ŭs), *pron.* (The letter "U"; an encompassing gesture.) The right "U" hand, palm facing the body, swings from right shoulder to left shoulder.

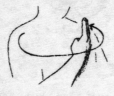

USE (*n.* ūs; *v.* ūz), *n.*, *v.*, USED, USING. (The letter "U.") The right "U" hand describes a small clockwise circle.

USE UP (ūz up), *v. phrase.* (Pull something off the hand.) The right "C" hand, palm facing left, is placed on the upturned left hand. The right hand, moving right, quickly leaves the left, while closing into a fist.

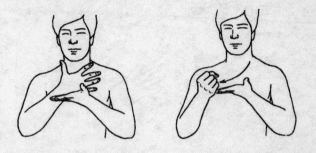

US TWO *phrase.* (Two persons interacting.) The right "V" hand, palm up and fingers pointing left, is swung in and out to and from the chest. *Also* WE TWO.

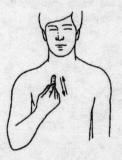

V

VACATION (vā kā′ shən), *n*. (A position of idleness.) With thumbs tucked in the armpits, the remaining fingers of both hands wiggle.

VARIOUS (vâr′ ĭ əs), *adj*. (The fingertips indicate many things.) Both hands, in the "D" position, palms out and index fingertips touching, are drawn apart. As they move apart, the index fingers wiggle up and down.

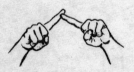

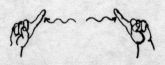

VCR *n.* (A fingerspelled loan sign.) The signer fingerspells "V-C-R."

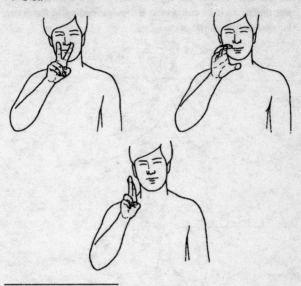

VERY (věr′ ĭ), *adv.* (The "V" hands, with the sign for MUCH.) The fingertips of the "V" hands are placed together, and then moved apart.

VIDEOTAPE (vid′ ē ō tāp), *n., v.* (The turning of the tape.) The left hand is held open, palm facing right. The right "V" hand makes a circle around the left palm, ending in the letter "T," and resting on the palm.

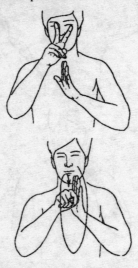

VIEW (vū), *n., v.,* VIEWED, VIEWING. (Look around.) The sign for LOOK is made: The right "V" hand, palm facing the body, is placed so that the fingertips are just under the eyes. Then both "V" hands are held with palms down and fingers pointing forward in front of the body. In this position the hands move simultaneously from side to side several times.

VISIT (vĭz′ĭt), *n., v.,* -ITED, -ITING. (The letter "V"; random movement, *i.e.,* moving around as in visiting.) The "V" hands, palms facing, move alternately in clockwise circles out from the chest.

VOTE (vōt), *n., v.,* VOTED, VOTING. (Placing a ballot in a box.) The right hand, holding an imaginary ballot between the thumb and index finger, places it into an imaginary box formed by the left "O" hand, palm facing right. *Also* ELECT.

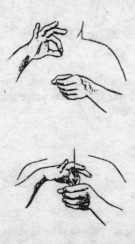

W

WAIT (wāt), *n.*, *v.*, WAITED, WAITING. (The fingers wiggle with impatience.) The upturned "5" hands are positioned with the right behind the left. The fingers of both hands wiggle.

WAIVE (wāv), *v.* (A wiped off and clean slate.) The right hand wipes off the left palm several times.

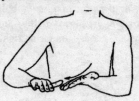

WALK (wôk), *n.*, *v.*, WALKED, WALKING. (The movement of the feet.) The downturned "5" hands move alternately toward and away from the chest.

WALLET *n.* (Placing the bills in.) The little finger edge of the open right hand, palm facing the body, is slipped into the

space created by the thumb and other fingers of the left hand.
The signer then mimes placing the wallet into a back pocket.

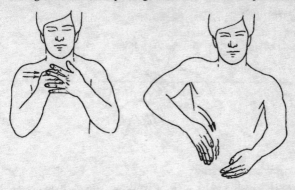

WANT (wŏnt, wônt), *v.*, WANTED, WANTING. (Grasping something and pulling it in.) The upturned "5" hands, held side by side before the chest, close slightly into a grasping position as they move in toward the body. *Also* DESIRE.

WARM (wôrm), *adj.*, *v.*, WARMED, WARMING. (The warmth of the breath is indicated.) The upturned cupped right hand is placed at the slightly open mouth. It moves up and away from the mouth, opening into the upturned "5" position, with fingers somewhat curved.

WARN (wôrn),*v.*, WARNED, WARNING. (Tapping one to draw attention to danger.) The right hand taps the back of the left several times.

WASH (wŏsh, wôsh), *n.*, *v.*, WASHED, WASHING. (Rubbing the clothes.) The knuckles of the "A" hands rub against one another, in circles.

WASH DISHES *v. phrase.* (The natural sign.) The downturned right "5" hand describes a clockwise circle as it moves over the upturned left "5" hand.

WASTE (wăst), *n.*, *v.*, WASTED, WASTING. (Repeated giving forth.) The back of the upturned right hand, thumb touching fingertips, is placed in the upturned left palm. The right hand moves off and away from the left once or several times, each time opening into the "5" position, palm up.

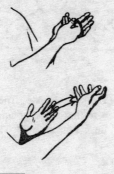

WATCH (wŏch), *n.* (The shape of the wristwatch.) The thumb and index finger of the right hand, forming a circle, are placed on the back of the left wrist.

WATER (wô′ tər, wŏt′ ər), *n.* (The letter "W" at the mouth, as in drinking water.) The right "W" hand, palm facing left, touches the lips a number of times.

WE (wē; *unstressed* wĭ), *pron.* (An encompassing movement.) The right index finger points down as it swings over from the right shoulder to the left shoulder.

WEAK (wĕk), *adj.* (The knees buckle.) The right "V" hand is placed with fingertips resting in the upturned left palm. The knuckles of the "V" fingers buckle a bit. This motion may be repeated.

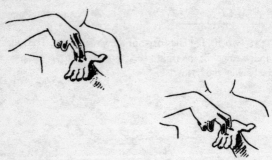

WEALTH (wĕlth), *n.* (A pile of money.) The sign for MONEY is made: The back of the upturned right hand, whose thumb and fingertips are all touching, is placed in the upturned left palm. The right hand then moves straight up, as it opens into the "5" position, palm facing down and fingers somewhat curved.

WEATHER (weŧh′ ər), *n.* (The letter "W.") The right "W" hand, palm out, moves straight down before the body, trembling slightly as it does.

WEDDING (wĕd′ ĭng), *n.* (A joining of hands.) The down-turned "B" hands are joined together with a flourish.

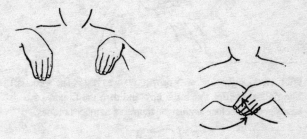

WEEK (wĕk), *n.* The upright, right "D" hand is placed palm-to-palm against the left "5" hand, whose palm faces right. The right "D" hand moves along the left palm from base to finger-tips.

WEIGH (wā), *v.*, WEIGHED, WEIGHING. (The balancing of the scale is described.) The fingers of the right "H" hand are centered on the left index finger and rocked back and forth.

WE'LL SEE *phrase*. (Modified from the sign for SEE.) The index finger of the right "V" hand, palm facing left, is placed at the corner of the right eye. The hand makes several very small back and forth movements. This is often accompanied by a very slight nodding.

WET (wĕt), *adj., n., v.*, WET or WETTED, WETTING. (The wetness.) The right fingertips touch the lips, and then the fingers of both hands open and close against the thumbs a number of times.

WE TWO *phrase*. (Two people interacting.) The right "V" hand, palm up and fingers pointing left, is swung in and out to and from the chest. *Also* US TWO.

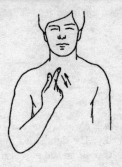

WHALE (hwāl), *n.* (The blowhole.) The right hand, in the AND position, fingers pointing up, is placed on top of the head. It moves up off the head and opens into the "5" position, representing the whale blowing out through the blowhole.

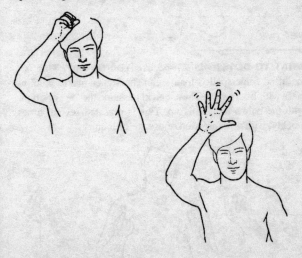

WHAT (hwŏt, hwŭt; *unstressed* hwət), *pron., adj., adv., interj., conj.* (The finger passes over several specifics to bring out the concept of "which one?") The right index finger passes over the fingers of the upturned left "5" hand, from index to little finger.

WHAT FOR? *(colloq.), phrase.* (For-For-For?) The sign for FOR is made repeatedly: The right index finger, resting on the right temple, leaves its position and moves straight out in front of the face. The sign is usually accompanied by an expression of inquiry, or annoyance.

WHAT TO DO? *(colloq.), phrase.* (Do-Do-Do?) This is a modified fingerspelled loan sign. The signer makes palm-up "D"s with both hands. These quickly assume the "O" position, with the palms remaining up. This is repeated several times, quickly, with an expression of despair or inquiry.

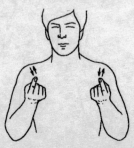

WHEN (hwĕn), *adv., conj., n.* (Fixing a point in time.) The left "D" hand is held upright, palm facing the body. The right index finger describes a clockwise circle around the left, coming to rest on the left index fingertip.

WHERE (hwâr), *adv.* (Alternate directions are indicated.) The right "D" hand, with palm out and index finger straight or slightly curved, moves a short distance back and forth, from left to right.

WHISPER (hwis′ pər), *n., v.* (Two people talk back and forth.) The right index and middle fingers rest on the lips. They individually go back and forth repeatedly striking the lips.

WHO (hōō), *pron.* (The pursed lips are indicated.) The right index finger traces a small counterclockwise circle in front of the lips, which are pursed in the enunciation of the word.

WHOSE (hōōz), *pron.* (Who; outstretched open hand signifies possession, as if pressing an item against the chest of the person spoken to.) The sign for WHO is made: The right index finger traces a small counterclockwise circle in front of the lips, which are pursed in the enunciation of the word. Then the right "5" hand, palm facing out, moves straight out toward the person spoken to or about.

WHY (hwī), *adv., n., interj.* (Reason--coming from the mind -- modified by the letter "Y," the phonetic equivalent of WHY.) The fingertips of the right hand, palm facing the body, are placed against the forehead. The right hand then moves down and away from the forehead, assuming the "Y" position, palm still facing the body. Expression is an important indicator of the context in which this sign is used. Thus, as an interjection, a severe expression is assumed; while as an adverb or a noun, the expression is blank or inquisitive.

WIDE (wīd), *adj.* (The width is indicated.) The open hands, fingers pointing out and palms facing each other, separate from their initial position an inch or two apart.

WIFE (wīf), *n.* (A female whose hand is clasped in marriage.) The FEMALE root sign is made: The thumb of the right "A" hand moves down along the right jawbone, almost to the chin. The hands are then clasped together, right above left.

Wind 256

WIND (wĭnd), *n.* (The blowing back and forth of the wind.) The "5" hands, palms facing and held up before the body, sway gracefully back and forth, in unison. The cheeks meanwhile are puffed up and the breath is being expelled. The nature of the swaying movement--graceful and slow, fast and violent, etc.--determines the type of wind. The strength of exhalation is also a qualifying device.

WINDOW (wĭn' dō), *n.* (The opening of the window.) With both palms facing the body, the little finger edge of the right hand rests atop the index finger edge of the left hand. The right hand then moves straight up and down.

WINDSURFING *n.* (The natural movement.) The signer, standing on an imaginary windsurfer and grasping the boom, executes a series of swaying maneuvers, as if guiding a surfboard.

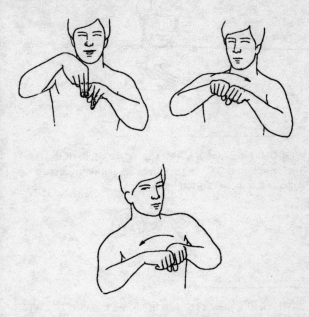

WINE (wīn), *n.* (The "W" hand indicates a flushed cheek.) The right "W" hand, palm facing the face, rotates at the right cheek, in either a clockwise or a counterclockwise direction.

WIPE (wīp), *v.* (Wiping with a cloth or towel.) The flattened right hand makes a series of clockwise wiping movements against the open left palm.

WISDOM (wĭz′ dəm), *n.* (Measuring the depth of the mind.) The downturned "X" finger moves up and down a short distance as it rests on mid-forehead.

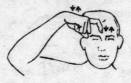

WITH (wĭth), *prep.* (The two hands are together, *i.e.*, WITH each other.) Both "A" hands, knuckles together and thumbs up, are moved forward in unison, away from the chest. They may also remain stationary.

WITHOUT (wĭth out′, with-), *prep., adv.* (The hands fall away from the WITH position.) The sign for WITH is formed.

The hands then drop down, open, and part, ending in the palms-down position.

WOMAN (wŏŏm′ ən), *n*. (A big female.) The FEMALE prefix sign is made: The thumb of the right "A" hand moves down along the line of the right jaw, from ear almost to chin. This outlines the string used to tie ladies' bonnets in olden days. This is a root sign to modify many others. The downturned right hand then moves up to a point above the head, to indicate the relative height.

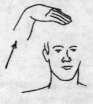

WONDER (wŭn′ dər), *v*., -DERED, -DERING. (Turning thoughts over in the mind.) Both index fingers, pointing to the forehead, describe continuous alternating circles.

WORD (wûrd), *n*. (A small part of a sentence, *i.e.*, a word.) The tips of the right index finger and thumb, about an inch apart, are placed on the side of the outstretched left index finger, which represents the length of a sentence.

WORD PROCESSING *n*. (A fingerspelled loan sign.) The signer fingerspells "W-P."

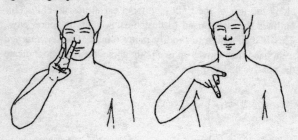

WORK (wûrk), *n., v.*, WORKED, WORKING. (Striking an anvil.) Both "S" hands are held palms down. The right hand strikes against the back of the left a number of times. *Also* JOB.

WORLD (wûrld), *n*. (The letter "W" in orbit.) The right "W" hand makes a complete circle around the left "W" hand and comes to rest on the thumb edge of the left "W" hand. The left hand frequently assumes the "S" position instead of the "W," to represent the stationary sun.

___

WOW! (wou), *interj.* The limp right hand is shaken up and down repeatedly, while the signer assumes a look of open mouthed surprise.

___

WRAP (rap), *v., n.* (Wrapping up a package.) Both down-turned hands, fingers pointing to each other, make a series of alternate clockwise circles, as if spreading wrapping paper around an object.

WRITE (rīt), *v.*, WROTE, WRITTEN, WRITING. (The natural movement.) The right index finger and thumb, grasping an imaginary pen, write across the open left palm.

X, Y, Z

XEROX (zǐr′ ŏks), *n.* (The letter "X"; the movement of the light as it moves under the item to be copied.) The "X" finger moves back and forth rather rapidly under the downturned hand.

YEAR (yǐr), *n.* (A circumference around the sun.) The right "S" hand, palm facing left, represents the earth. It is positioned atop the left "S" hand, whose palm faces right, and represents the sun. The right "S" hand describes a clockwise circle around the left, coming to rest in its original position.

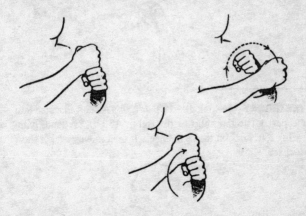

YEAR-ROUND *adj.* (Making a revolution around the sun.) The right index finger, resting on the left index, goes forward around the left once, coming back to where it began.

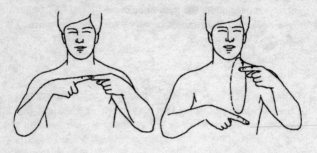

YES (yĕs), *(colloq.)*, *adv.*, *n.* (The nodding.) The right "S" hand, imitating the head, "nods" up and down.

YESTERDAY (yĕs′ tər dĭ, -dā′), *adv.*, *n.* (A short distance into the past.) The thumbtip of the right "A" or "Y" hand, palm facing left, rests on the right cheek. It then moves back a short distance.

YOU (ū), *pron. sing.* (The natural sig*n*.) The signer points to the person he is addressing.

YOUNG (yŭng), *adj.* (The spirits bubbling up.) The fingertips of both open hands, placed on either side of the chest just below the shoulders, move up and off the chest, in unison, to a point just above the shoulders. This is repeated several times.

YOUR (yŏŏr), *pron., adj.* (The outstretched open hand indicates possession, as if pressing an item against the chest of the person spoken to.) The right "5" hand, palm facing out, moves straight out toward the person spoken to.

YOURSELF (yŏŏr sĕlf′), *pron.* The signer moves his upright thumb in the direction of the person spoken to.

YOURSELVES (yŏŏr sĕlvz′), *pron. pl.* The signer moves his upright thumb toward several people before him, in a series of small forward movements from left to right.

ZERO (zĭr′ ŏ), *(colloq.), n.* (An emphatic movement of the "O," *i.e.,* ZERO, hand.) The little finger edge of the right "O" hand is brought sharply into the upturned left palm.

REPRESENTATIVE PHRASES AND SENTENCES

Author's Note: Some sentences and phrases, where feasibility and usage play roles, are given in traditional ASL sign order; some are given in more English-like word order or gloss.

Appropriate facial expression, pacing, personal projection of the signer, eye contact, etc., are key elements in successful signing. When asking a question, the signer traditionally furrows the brow, raises the eyebrows, or both. The body may lean forward an inch or two. A question mark is frequently drawn in the air, to lend emphasis.

Certain material may be omitted. Pronouns, articles, the verb *to be*, frequently superfluous or redundant in ASL, are examples. A noun sign repeated (reduplication) usually means the plural of that noun. Example: *friend friend=friends.* Likewise, repeating a verb sign can change it to a noun. Example: *fly* repeated becomes *airplane.*

ASL tenses are usually understood in context. An ASL example: "I recently get (a) letter" becomes "got (a) letter" due to the time-setting function of "recently," which sets the time in the past.

I accept your advice.

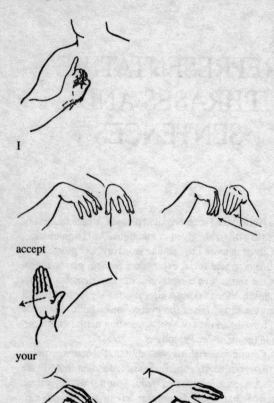

I

accept

your

advice

Can you tell me why?

Can

you

tell me

why

I have enough money.
(Money enough have)

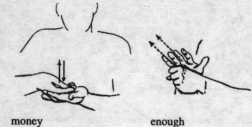

money   enough

have

Sorry, I wasn't born yesterday.
(Sorry, born yesterday not)

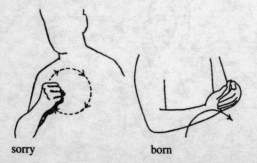

sorry   born

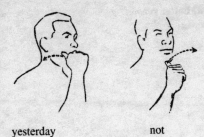

yesterday   not

I don't want to replace them.
(*Them   replace   don't   want*)

them

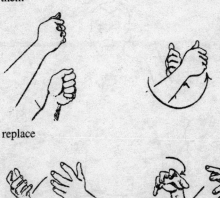

replace

don't want

You must look for *[a]* better reason.

you

must

look for

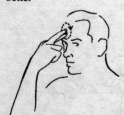

better

reason

You should change your pants.
(*Pants   your   change   should*)

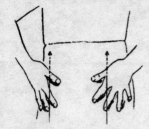

pants

your

change

should

I recently got [a] letter from your grandmother.

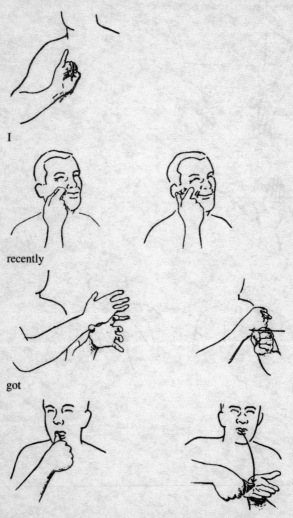

I

recently

got

letter

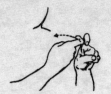

from

your

grandmother

We have many interests in common.
(We have many interests in [same].)

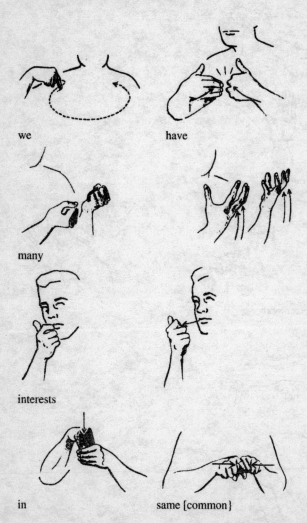

we

have

many

interests

in

same [common]

I'm not comfortable about that new doctor.
(*Comfortable   not   about   new   doctor   there.*)

comfortable

not

about   new

doctor

there

(I) must buy (a) stamp for (the) letter.

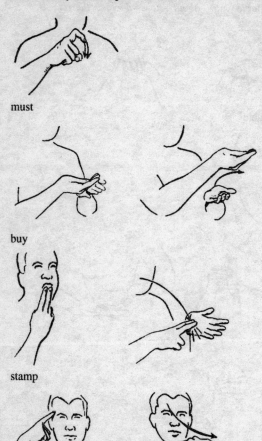

must

buy

stamp

for

letter

What time is it?
(*Time?*)

time

(I) don't want (to) inform them till next week.

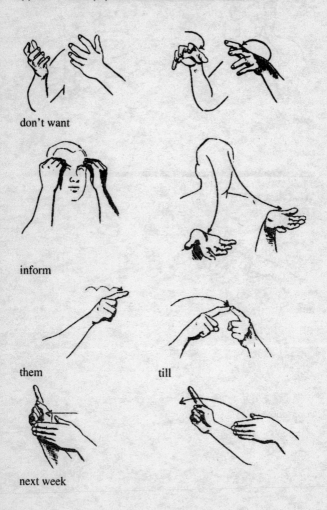

don't want

inform

them   till

next week

I'm crazy about the new automobile.
(*Automobile   new   (me)   crazy   about.*)

automobile

new

crazy about

Have (you) seen (the) new film?
(See finish new film question mark)

see

finish

new

film

question mark

(The) new computer arrived. I'm excited.
(*Computer new arrive succeed. Excite me.*)

computer

new

arrive

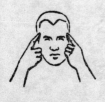   

succeed

(continued)

exite

me

(I) don't want (to) excuse that stupid mistake.

don't want

excusxe   that

stupid   mistake

My niece was recently divorced.

(*Recently   niece   mine   divorce.*)

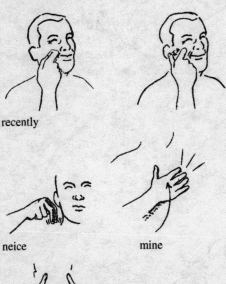

recently

neice   mine

divorce

We have (a) real desire (to) see you again.

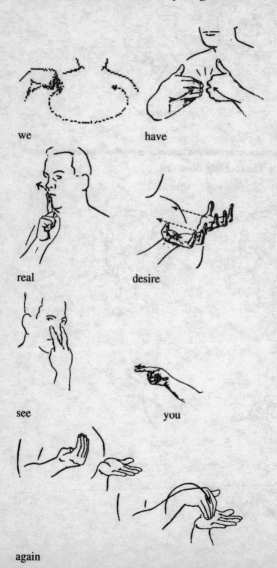

we

have

real

desire

see

you

again

I'm lonely without our dog.

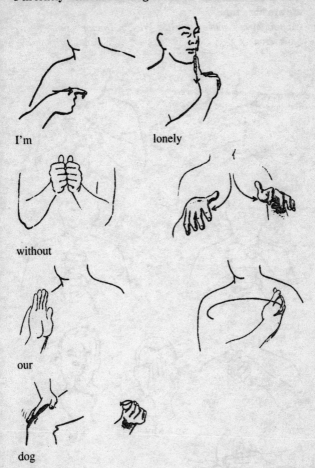

I'm   lonely

without

our

dog

You must make an appointment. The doctor doesn't always have time.

(Appointment make must. Why? Doctor not always have time.)

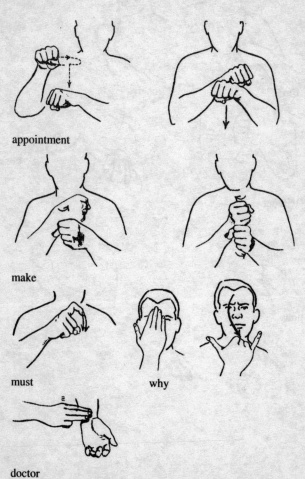

appointment

make

must   why

doctor

not

always

have

time

You're (a) selfish person. You never think about your friends.

you're

selfish

person

you

never

think

about

your

friends

friends

I'm shocked. Why? You forgot (to) bring my book.

(Shocked me. Why? Forget you bring book mine.)

shocked

me

why

forget

you

bring

book

mine

(I) don't know what (to) do with that money.

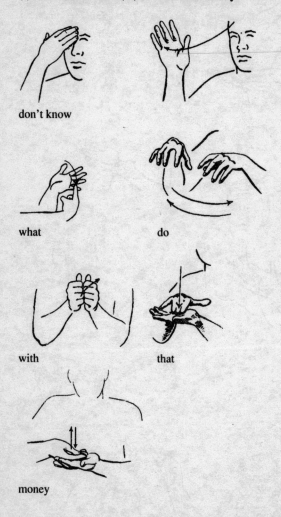

don't know

what   do

with   that

money

I know you suffered (a lot); now you finally smile.
(*I know   suffer suffer   you.   Now [you]   smile   succeed.*)

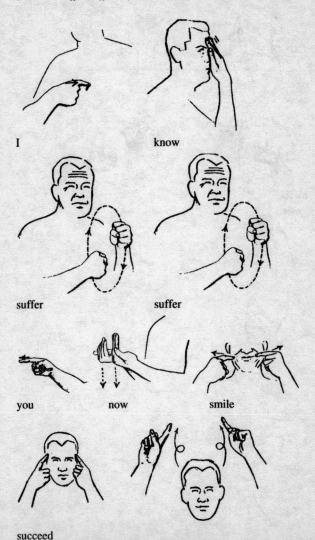

I   know

suffer   suffer

you   now   smile

succeed

Maybe I'm alone, but lonely, no.
(*Alone maybe yes, lonely no.*)

alone

maybe

yes

lonely

no

(That's) right! (I) remember you.

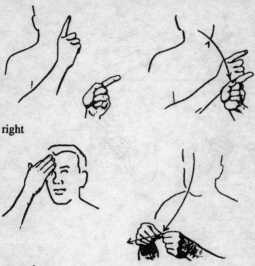

right

remember

you

Can you remain with me today?

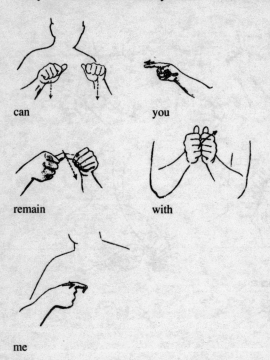

can

you

remain

with

me

today

Yes, (I) know, but (I) don't understand why.

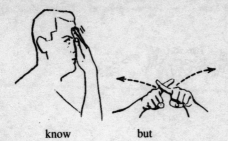

yes   know   but

don't

understand

why

I have a few cats under the house.
(*Cat cat few have. Where? Under house.*)

cat

cat

few   have

where

under

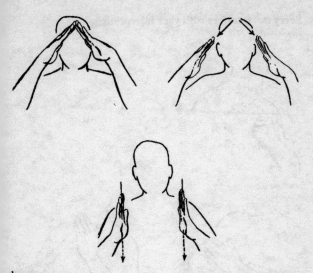

house

(You) seem thin. Why?

seem

thin   why

Sorry (to) interfere with your interpreting.

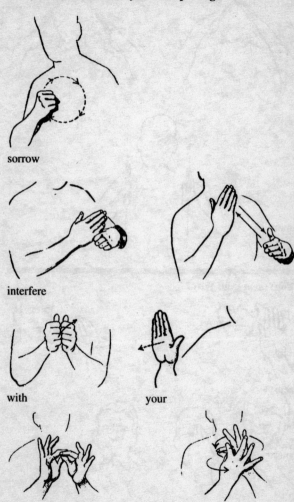

sorrow

interfere

with

your

interpreting

(I) must buy more milk.
(*Milk   more   buy   must.*)

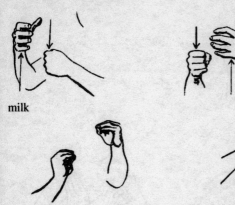

milk

more

buy

must

Yesterday (my) wife told me (she) wants (a) new baby.

yesterday

wife

told me

wants

new

baby

You must inform (the) family about our recent marriage.

you

must

inform

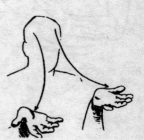

family

about

our

recent

marriage

Do I want a new coat? No.
(*Me   want   coat   new   question mark.   No.*)

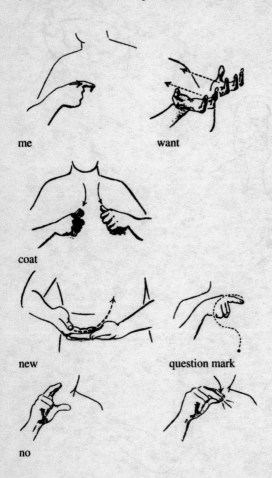

me   want

coat

new   question mark

no

I always enjoy teaching young children.

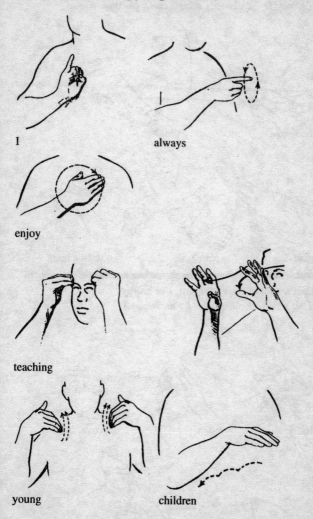

I   always

enjoy

teaching

young   children

Can you encourage my children?
(*Encourage   children   mine   can   question mark.*)

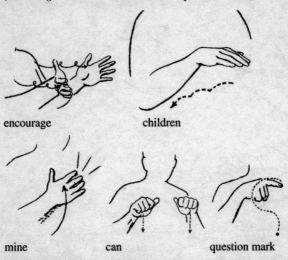

encourage   children

mine   can   question mark

That's a lot of improvement. I'm happy.
(*That's   much   improve.   I'm   happy.*)

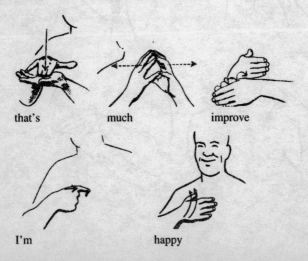

that's   much   improve

I'm   happy

Why are you late? You never arrive on time.
(*Why   late   question mark.   (You)   never   arriv(al)   right time.*)

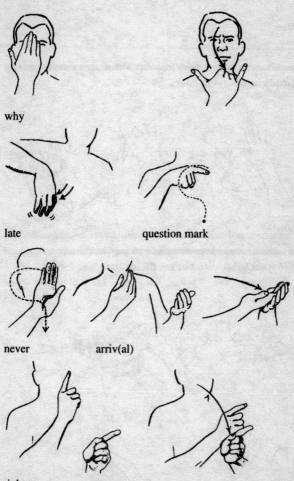

why

late   question mark

never   arriv(al)

right

(continued)

time

Goodbye. See (you) later.

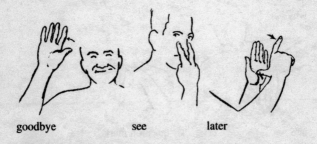

goodbye   see   later

We want to see you, but not till my daughter leaves.
(*We want see (you), but not till daughter mine leaves.*)

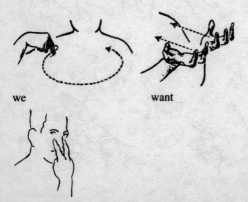

we   want

see

but

not

till

daughter   mine

leaves

Wow! You're finished. I'm surprised.

wow

you're

finished

I'm

surprised

Those kids have already become snobs.]
(Kids   there   finish   change to   snob(s).)

kids

there

finish

change to

snob(s)

Sign language allows deaf people to talk (with) ease.
(*Sign language   permission   deaf   said   easy.*)

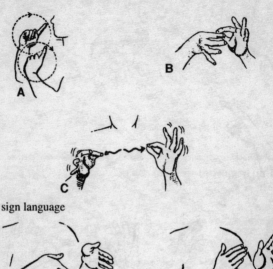

sign language

permission

deaf

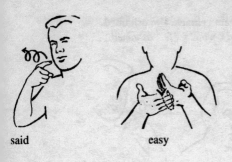

said   easy

Hi! (I'm) happy (to) see (you) again.
(*Hello!*)

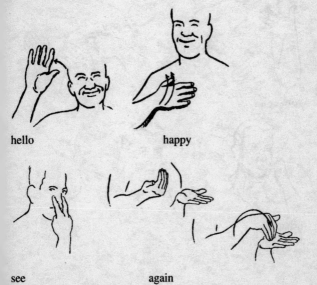

hello   happy

see   again

What an ignorant remark. I'm ashamed.
(*Ignorant said wow! Me ashamed.*)

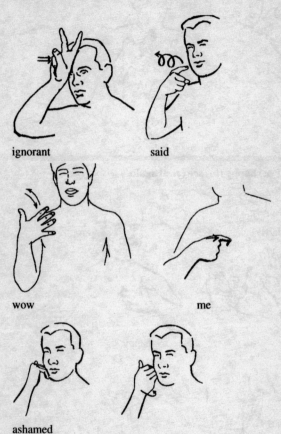

ignorant said

wow me

ashamed

I rely regular(ly) on children [mine] for help.

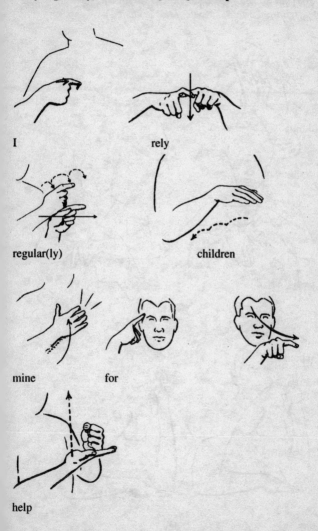

I   rely

regular(ly)   children

mine   for

help

During early school days I saw them a lot.
(During early school day day me finish see them much.)

during

early

school

day   day

me

finish

see them

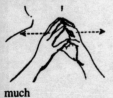

much

Hello. We just arrived here.

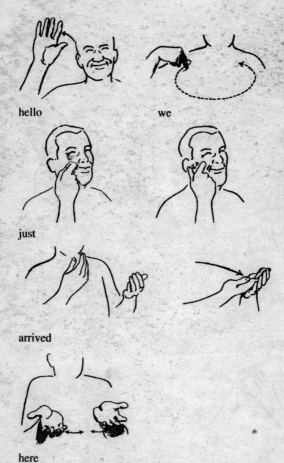

hello

we

just

arrived

here